PROGRESSING THROUGH CHESS

PROGRESSING THROUGH CHESS:
THE THIRTY-FIVE BEST CHESS BOOKS AND HOW TO USE THEM

JOHN GREFE
INTERNATIONAL MASTER

PLAYERS PRESS
LOS ANGELES

ABOUT THE AUTHOR

John Grefe is thirty-four years old and lives in Berkeley, California. A tournament chessplayer since the age of fifteen, he gained a candidate master's rating after only four rated tournaments. He and grandmaster Lubomir Kavalek shared the U.S. Champion's title in 1973, and in 1975 FIDE, the International Chess Federation, awarded Mr. Grefe the International Master title. Winner of numerous tournaments, two of his most recent victories were the 1980 American Open and the 1981 Northern California State Championship, the strongest state championship ever held in America.

Mr. Grefe is also the author of *The Best of Lone Pine*, published by RHM.

ACKNOWLEDGMENTS
Thanks are due to Alan Benson for making his chess library available for research, and to Rainer Rickford for help and encouragement. Also to Randall Hough, Kent Smith and Dia Hauser for their work in the production and proofreading of the ms.

Published by The Players Press, 1710 Silver Lake Boulevard,
Los Angeles, California 90026

ISBN 0-941426-01-7 Paperback
Manufactured in the United States of America

Chess, like love, like music,
has the power to make men happy.
...GM (Grandmaster) Siegbert Tarrasch

What is true happiness? Only the
Perfect Master knows, and he makes people
happy by revealing
the never-ending fountain of bliss
hidden in their hearts.
...PM (Perfect Master) Guru Maharaj Ji

CONTENTS

PREFACE:
A FEW NOTES
ABOUT RECORDING
GAMES

TWO SYSTEMS of notation, English descriptive and algebraic, currently enjoy worldwide popularity. You will need to learn them both for study, but I recommend that you use algebraic to record your games.

Today, most chess books are printed in algebraic because it is more efficient and compact. English publishers cut costs and appeal to the widest possible market by using algebraic, for this is the system preferred by the vast majority of Europeans.

Mastering notation is important. Otherwise, when you play over games, you will frequently find yourself studying the wrong position or wasting time trying to locate squares. Quick identification of squares promotes clear thinking and confidence. Masters rarely make scorekeeping errors, but their weaker brethren sin often. Practice naming squares until you can identify them instantly.

a8	b8	c8	d8	e8	f8	g8	h8
a7	b7	c7	d7	e7	f7	g7	h7
a6	b6	c6	d6	e6	f6	g6	h6
a5	b5	c5	d5	e5	f5	g5	h5
a4	b4	c4	d4	e4	f4	g4	h4
a3	b3	c3	d3	e3	f3	g3	h3
a2	b2	c2	d2	e2	f2	g2	h2
a1	b1	c1	d1	e1	f1	g1	h1

In algebraic notation, each square has a single designation. . .

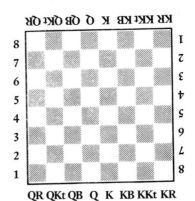

QR QKt QB Q K KB KKt KR

while English descriptive notation features separate designations for Black and White.

In English descriptive, each square has two names. One speaks of moves from White's vantage point, the other from Black's. The squares have only one name in algebraic.

Horizontal rows of squares are called ranks. White's first rank, along which his pieces are aligned at the start of the game, is Black's eighth rank; his second is Black's seventh, etc. Vertical rows of squares are called files. The file to White's left is the Queen's Rook file; next comes the Queen's Knight file. The file on his far right is the King's Rook file. In algebraic we have the *a - file, b - file*, etc.

:

(The symbol "e.p." for "en passant" is not used at all in algebraic; it also permits slight variations, such as omitting the letter "P" for Pawn moves, and so on.)

SYMBOLS

P . . . . *Pawn*
N . . . . *Knight*
B . . . . *Bishop*
R . . . . *Rook*
Q . . . .*Queen*
K . . . . *King*
"x" or ":" . . . . *captures*
" — " . . . .*to*
"†"or "ch" . . . . *check*
(Q) . . . . . . *promotes to a Queen*
0-0 . . . . . .*castles Kingside (short)*
(W) . . . . *White to move*
(B) . . . . *Black to move*
0-0-0 . . *castles Queenside (long)*
e.p. . . . .*captures* **en passant**
! . . . . *good move*
!! . . . . *fantastic move*
!? . . . . . *risky, enterprising move; a move deserving consideration*
?! . . . . *a dubious but imaginative move*
? . . . . *a mistake*
?? . . . .*a horrible blunder*
X . . . . *checkmate*
½—½ . . . .*draw*
1—0 (48) . . . . . *White won in 48 moves*

ENGLISH DESCRIPTIVE		LONG ALGEBRAIC		ALGEBRAIC	
1 P–K4	P–QB4	e2–e4	c7–c5	e4	c5
2 N–KB3	N–QB3	Ng1–f3	Nb8–c6	Nf3	Nc6
3 P–Q4	PxP	d2–d4	c5xd4	d4	cxd4
4 NxP	N–B3	Nf3xd4	Ng8–f6	Nxd4	Nf6
5 N–QB3	P–Q3	Nb1–c3	d7–d6	Nc3	d6
6 B–KN5	P–QR3	Bc1–g5	a7–a6	Bg5	a6
7 Q–Q2	N–Q2	Qd1–d2	Nf6–d7	Qd2	Nd7
8 B–K2	P–KN3	Bf1–e2	g7–g6	Be2	g6
9 N–Q5	P–B3	Nc3–d5	f7-f6	Nd5	f6
10 N–K6	Q–R4	Nd4–e6	Qd8–a5	Ne6	Qa5
11 N(Q5)-B7ch	K–B2	Nd5–c7+	Ke8–f7	Ndc7+	Kf7
12 N–Q8ch	K–N2	Ne6–d8+	Kf7–g7	Nd8+	Kg7
13 N–K8ch	RESIGNS	Nc7–e8+	1 – 0	Ne8+	1 – 0

Kluger-Nagy
Budapest 1942

The scores above are read:

English Descriptive: "Pawn to King four; Pawn to Queen's Bishop four.
Knight to King's Bishop three; Knight to Queen's Bishop three.
Pawn to Queen four; Pawn takes Pawn."

Long Algebraic: "Pawn at e2 to e4; Pawn at c7 to c5. Knight at g1 to
f3; Knight at b8 to c6. Pawn at d2 to d4; Pawn at c5 takes on d4."

Algebraic: "e4; c5. Knight to f3; Knight to c6. d4; c takes d4."

3

INTRODUCTION

THIS BOOK is for anyone who wants to play better chess. Systematic and comprehensive, it is a pragmatic guide to the study and application of our accumulated knowledge about chess. Absolute beginners and budding masters alike will find it an effective tool for sharpening their skills. *While it is designed for the ambitious player, its methods can be adapted to fit a more modest approach to the game.*

After reviewing hundreds of books, I selected thirty-five (more, counting multi-volume works) that I consider to be the very best ever written. Aimed at all classes of players, they encompass every aspect of practical play. These books contain everything that anyone would need to learn in order to become a formidably strong chess player. I built the framework of this book around them.

Popular fancy holds that chess is an abstruse, intellectual exercise suitable primarily for eccentric geniuses and egomaniacs. Not only have recent world championship matches not dispelled this notion, they have reinforced it. Flamboyant personalities and outrageous political and psychological hi-jinks captured headlines around the globe, thrusting chess and chessmasters dramatically into public view.

Folk mythology not withstanding, chess is fairly easy to understand. No concept in chess lies beyond the grasp of the average person; anyone can learn how to play in a few hours.

Mastering chess, however, is another matter entirely. Hard work and dedication, as in any serious endeavor, are indispensable. You might well ask, "If chess is relatively easy to understand, why is it difficult to master?" The answer lies in the vast scope of the game.

The number of different positions that can arise is astronomical. Chess theory tackles this problem by classifying moves, positions, and their underlying ideas. The number of these is, by comparison, extremely small. Every year thousands of fascinating games are played throughout the world, but virtually all of them consist of patterns and ideas already known. They merely appear in novel settings.

This book represents the first attempt to incorporate all chess theory into a systematic course of study. Its byword is specialization.

Specialization means developing a personalized study program tailored to our playing strength, temperament and resources. It means systematic study focusing on the ideas and types of positions most likely to arise in our own games. And it means solving exercises that will develop our playing skills, enabling us to transform the frog of theory into the prince of practice at a single stroke.

I have attempted to solve the problem of appealing to a broad spectrum of players by deliberately selecting simple positions to illustrate certain points, and ask the stronger players to bear with me on this matter. No one is ignored, however. Throughout the book are hints and suggestions for every class of player.

Chapter One answers the question, *"What Do We Need to Learn?"* -- by analyzing some basic chess positions and breaking them down into their component parts.

Chapter Two contains numerous study tips and shows how to develop a personal study program.

Chapter Three recommends the order in which each class of players should study the "thirty-five best books."

Chapter Four looks at the books themselves. It introduces each one, highlights its most valuable assets, and where necessary provides additional explanatory material, questions, and exercises.

Chapter Five is unique. It summarizes all of the key ideas in chess, in the form of review tables illustrated by diagrams and supplemented by exercises. These tables place the essence of chess at your fingertips. When reviewed before a tournament, they quickly bring key concepts to the forefront of consciousness.

Rounding out this work are two cross-referenced lists of books. The first contains the collected games of the world's best players, past and present. These games constitute the very heart of chess theory and practice. Referring to them as you study a particular phase of chess will bring inspiration and enlightenment. They demonstrate how the titans of chess dispatched their rivals by applying the very same ideas that you are studying.

The second list offers books for further reading, or those not included among the "thirty-five best books" for various reasons. Outstanding books are noted so that players already possessing them may substitute them, if they so desire, for books on the "thirty-five best" list.

Very few books written for beginners and lower-rated players promote real understanding. The knowledge they need to gain this understanding exists, but being interwoven with more sophisticated ideas in books intended for advanced players it remains beyond reach. This material has been unraveled, and can be found scattered throughout *The 35 Best Chess Books*.

Despite the vast array of chess books, certain areas of the game remain relatively unexplored. This is especially true of the subjective side of chess — the masters' thought processes. I hope you will join me when I chart some of this terrain in my next book for the Players Press — *Thinking Techniques for the Tournament Player*.

International Master
JOHN GREFE

THE THIRTY-FIVE
BEST CHESS BOOKS
AND WHO SHOULD
USE THEM

	Novice Cat. IV 1200-1399	Cat. III 1400-1599	Cat. II 1600-1799	Cat. I 1800-1999	Cand. Master 2000-2199
1) A Programmed Introduction to the Game of Chess	X				
2) Learn Chess: A New Way for All					
Volume I — First Principles	X				
Volume II - Winning Methods	X	X			
3) Understanding the Open Games	X	X	X		
4) The Art of Chess Combination	X	X			
5) Essential Knowledge	X	X			
6) The 1000 Best Short Games of Chess	X	X	X	X	X
7) Art of the Checkmate	X	X	X		
8) Logical Chess Move by Move	X	X			
9) 1001 Brilliant Ways to Checkmate	X	X	X	X	X
1001 Winning Chess Sacrifices and Combinations	X	X	X	X	X
10) Illustrated Dictionary of Chess	X	X	X	X	X
11) Ideas Behind the Chess Openings		X	X	X	
12) Better Chess for Average Players		X	X		
13) Tactics of Endgames		X	X		
14) How to Play Chess Endings		X	X		
15) How to Open a Chess Game		X	X	X	
16) Practical Endgame Lessons			X	X	
17) Judgment and Planning in Chess			X	X	X
18) A Complete Defense to 1 P—K4			X	X	X
A Complete Defense to 1 d4			X	X	X
19) Modern Chess Tactics:					
Pieces and Pawns in Action			X	X	X
Attack and Defense			X	X	X
20) Modern Chess Strategy			X	X	X
21) Art of Attack in Chess			X	X	X
22) Pawn Structure Chess			X	X	X
23) Grandmaster of Chess: Paul Keres			X	X	X
24) 500 Master Games of Chess			X	X	X
25) Modern Chess Opening Theory			X	X	X
26) Chess Informant			X	X	X
27) Batsford, RHM, etc., opening books			X	X	X
28) Basic Chess Endings			X	X	X
29) Batsford endgame series			X	X	X
Rook Endings			X	X	X
30) Alekhine's Best Games:					
1908 - 1923; 1924 - 1937			X	X	X
31) The Best Move			X	X	X
32) Psychology in Chess			X	X	X
33) Think Like a Grandmaster			X	X	X
Play Like a Grandmaster			X	X	X
Train Like a Grandmaster			X	X	X
34) Grandmaster Preparation			X	X	X
35) Encyclopedia of Chess Openings				X	X

WHAT DO WE
NEED TO LEARN?

S T R I P P E D to its essentials, a game of chess is a chain of moves. It grows steadily, link by link, as the players alternately respond to one another's ploys. Each move brings a new position; each position brings a new move.

Moves are manifested thoughts. They are the treasures gathered on a journey that begins in the concrete world of pawns, pieces, and squares, and ends in the abstract realm of the mind.

Completing the journey takes three steps. First, the players repeatedly cast their gaze over the position, trying to discern its special features and relationships. Next, they organize this information. Finally, they choose their moves.

Analyzing some typical positions will reveal the actual content of their thoughts and observations.

The Kings stand in direct opposition when only one square separates them vertically, horizontally or diagonally. The player not on move "has the opposition." The rival King must give way unless he can seize the opposition himself (e.g., through a temporizing Pawn move.)

Only White can win this position. He plans to achieve his goal of checkmating the Black King by queening his Pawn. Black's goal is a draw.

White hopes to be able to utilize the opposition so that his King can support the advance of his Pawn. Black's arsenal includes the opposition, the blockade, and stalemate.

1 ... Ke6 2 Kd4 (White cannot maintain the opposition.) 2 ... Kd6 (Now it belongs to Black.) 3 e5† (This Pawn move regains the opposition for White.) 3 ... Ke6 4 Ke4 Ke7 (4 ... Kd7 and 4 ... Kf7 are also feasible. After 4 ... Kd7 5 Kd5 Ke7 6 e6 Ke8 7 Kd6 Kd8, we reach the main line.) 5 Kd5 Kd7 6 e6† Ke7 7 Ke5 (a critical position — Black has only one drawing move.) 7 ... Ke8! Surrendering the opposition now with 7 ... Kd8?? would lose after 8 Kd6 Ke8 9 e7, etc.) 8 Kd6 Kd8 9 e7† Ke8. If White refuses to abandon his Pawn, 10 Ke6 will stalemate the Black King.

The most elementary position in chess has supplied a partial answer to the query posed by the title of this chapter. We need to learn about plans and goals, methods and means.

This position is closely related to the previous ones. Although Black's Pawn is doomed, he may be able to salvage a draw.

Let's follow the course of his thoughts, which probably run something like this: "If I play 1 . . . Kg6, White will play 2 Kf4, his only sensible move. Then, if the game continues 2 . . . Kf6 3 Kxe4 Ke6, 4 Kf4 Kf6 5 f3 — he'll have the opposition and a winning position. I need to find something else."

Evaluating the above line as hopeless, Black shifts his search. "My only alternative is 1 . . . e3. If that doesn't work I've had it, though I'll still have to decide which move gives White the biggest headache. White must play 2 fxe3 — advancing his Pawn would be a colossal blunder that allows me to queen. What next? I've got to stop his Pawn, so 2 . . . Kg6 3 Kf4 Kf6 4 Ke4 Ke6. I've got the opposition for good! That's an easy draw."

Black had to analyze variations and evaluate positions in order to find the right moves. His success was strongly predicated upon knowledge of the inevitable outcome of certain positions (assuming best play on both sides.)

The cornered Black King and threatening White pieces participate in a beautifully choreographed dance of death.

1 Nf7† Kg8 2 Nh6† Kh8 3 Qg8†!! Rxg8 4 Nf7 mate. This well-known mate is called *Philidor's legacy* or a smothered mate.

The successful execution of White's maneuver required the fulfillment of certain conditions. Reversing the positions of Black's Queen and Rook, for example, would introduce the defensive resource 4 . . Qxf7.

Recurring piece patterns and outstanding features of the position may be tactical, as in the last example, or they may be strategical, as in the next.

1 b5! (Crippling the Black pawn majority. White, in effect, now has an extra Pawn. 1 g5? would only draw after 1 . . . c5.) 1 . . . Kf6 2 g5† hxg5 3 hxg5† Kg6 4 Kg4 Kg7 5 Kf5 Kf7 6 g6† (This Pawn will distract Black's King while White gobbles Pawns on the other wing.) 6 . . . Kg7 7 Ke6 Kxg6 8 Kd7, etc.

There is yet another method of handling and evaluating positions. We can break them down into their elements, weighing the pluses and minuses of each side. The elements are *time, space, material, pawn structure, king safety,* and the *initiative.* Each element is found in practically every position.

We encountered space and material in diagram 2; diagram 4 demonstrated the intimate relationship between time, the initiative, and king safety; and diagram 5 graphically brought home the advantages of a superior pawn structure.

Summary
*Every move should play an integral part in a plan designed to reach a particular goal.
*The most critical features of each position dictate the correct plan.
*Pattern recognition, useful in hitting upon the correct plan, plays a key role in evaluating all types of positions.
*Patterns may be strategical and/or tactical.
*There are six interrelated elements: time, space, material, pawn structure, king safety, and the initiative.
*We can evaluate positions by gauging the elements that affect them.
*The ability to calculate a series of moves, be it ever so short, is indispensable to every player.

What Do We Need To Learn?

— Plans and Goals — Recurring Patterns
— Methods and Means — Elements
-- Attack and Defense — How to Analyze Variations
— Strategy and Tactics — How to Evaluate Positions

STUDY HINTS

C H E S S   G A M E S begin in a state of equilibrium. The armies arrayed on the board mirror one another in every respect — make-up, firepower and battle stations. The *chances are balanced.* They will remain so unless one of the players makes a mistake, for *the balance cannot be upset by force.* If both players make good moves from start to finish, the game will end in a draw. Balanced positions always contain at least one good move that maintains the status quo.

As soon as one of the players makes a bad move, his opponent can tip the scales in his favor and attain a material or positional advantage by playing a good move. Once the chances become unbalanced, a continuous series of good moves by both players will keep them unbalanced. An error by the inferior side will give the opponent an opportunity to increase his advantage still further. An error by the superior side will permit the opponent to reduce his inferiority, equalize, or gain the upper hand. Thus there are varying degrees of good and bad moves.

Some positions contain only one good move. Most offer a choice of several equally alluring alternatives. Good moves and good positions naturally go hand-in-hand, though we may think more in terms of one rather than the other, depending on circumstances. Everything the practical player studies should be geared to developing the ability to find good moves and recognize good positions while avoiding bad moves and bad positions.

This requires a well-balanced study program that encompasses the opening, the middlegame, and the endgame. We need strategy and tactics in equal measure, and clear, methodical thinking with which to employ them.

Productive study requires motivation. Boris Spassky revealed that, several months prior to his world championship tussle with Bobby Fischer, he hung a picture of the American champion on his living room wall. Is there a player at your club that you are dying to beat? Do you want to become a Category I player? A master? World champion?

Keep your goal in sight. If you don't have one, find one. It will bring your study program sharply into focus, engender enthusiasm, and whet your appetite for chess. Be flexible. Your goals will probably change as you improve.

Charting your progress will lend further impetus to your endeavors. If you play in tournaments regularly, you can keep track of your rating in relation to the number of hours you study in, say, a one-month period. You can also chart your tournament results this way. Another approach is to solve a certain set of exercises, then return to them later and compare your results. If your progress slows, the chart can be useful in pinpointing the source of your difficulties.

The most important factors to consider when planning your study are your tastes, playing style, strength, goals, and perhaps most important, the amount of time available for study and play. A close look at the special problems involved in mastering each phase of the game will fill in some blanks.

THE OPENING
(Numbers in parentheses or brackets
refer to the 'thirty-five best books.' If preceded
by a Roman Numeral, they refer to
Supplementary List I or II.)

Category II players and below should begin with a solid grounding in the open games (see [3 and 11] for details). Once you have decided which openings to play, pick out a few main lines in each. Instead of simply trying to memorize columns of moves, however, pick out key positions between moves twelve and fifteen. You can use a diagram kit to record these positions on file cards, or even better, have your printer make up a sheets containing diagrams, and staple them together. This way you can easily keep track of positions with related ideas. On the back of each diagram write down the moves leading to the position. Then you can look at the position and try to work out the moves leading to it by playing them out on a board, or you can look at the moves and try to set up the position they lead to. Keep track of the time it takes to get a feel for about five main lines in one opening, and use this as a basis for deciding how much time to spend on the openings in general. The stronger you become, the more you will want to expand your repertoire and delve more deeply into each line. Always remember that moves represent ideas, and that each opening is really just a grouping of varitions with related ideas. (See [18] in order to gain a perspective on a viable repertoire. For further reading consult [15; I I - 2, 3, 4, 5, 7] .Players pressed for time may want to follow the suggestions in [I I - 6]). The ideal approach to *any* opening is illustrated by (I I - 1). Unfortunately, it is currently out of print.

THE MIDDLEGAME

In a sense, studying the openings is just looking up beforehand the specific moves you would have to spend time thinking about at the board. Middlegames, however, cannot be handled this way. In this area of the game, pattern recognition, positional judgment, tactical alertness and calculation play the starring roles.

Suggestions on the best ways to solve exercises can be found in (33). Probably the two most important books in this whole field are (22 and 33, Vol. I).

THE ENDGAME

Science rules in the endgame. Thousands of standard positions have been subjected to rigorous examination and classified according to their piece/pawn content and structure. Some of the most brilliant minds in chess have written outstanding works in this field.

Once we learn a few basic positions, techniques, and principles, it mainly becomes a question of expanding their number. (28) lists those endings which are essential to mastering this part of the game.

As with the opening, a set of file cards that can be quickly and easily reviewed is an effective tool. On the reverse of the diagrams (see 28) should be symbols indicating who wins and one or two main lines. In some of the more difficult Rook-and-Pawn endgames, you may want to make up several diagrams in order to chart the progression of key positions.

GENERAL ADVICE

This book has been designed along comprehensive lines to benefit the serious player. Adopt only those suggestions you feel comfortable with; alter them to suit yourself.

Keep notebooks of unusual positions, opening ideas, and questions that arise during your studies.

Chess games cannot be won if somebody doesn't make a mistake. Ten of the world's best players, all battle-scarred veterans with international tournament victories to their credit, gathered at the Tournament of Stars in Montreal, 1979. Thirty-six of the ninety games they played ended decisively. The moral: even the best players make many mistakes, so don't be overly concerned about yours.

Eliminating the weak spots in your play demands an objective appraisal of your games.

Category II players and below are advised to set up positions on their boards when studying, rather than relying solely on diagrams.

If you cannot figure out the reason behind a move, or if it seems impossible, make sure you're looking at the right position! The first step in solving exercises should be to assess the material situation.

Be forewarned that chess books contain their fair share of typographic errors and incorrect evaluations of positions.

Don't look up the answers to exercises until you have made your very best effort to solve them.

Don't try to memorize anything unless you enjoy doing so. Important ideas can be assimilated more effectively by trying to apply them again and again in varying circumstances.

The review tables can be used at any time by any player.

Although Chapter Three presents the "thirty-five best books" on the basis of ratings, it's mostly a matter of making do with what's available. Ratings reflect long- and short-term trends, not a player's strengths and weaknesses. A Category I player, for example, might not be over-rated, but he may understand very little about Rook-and-Pawn endings. If he suddenly found himself on the losing side of a couple of them, in the same tournament against lower-rated opposition, he'd be likely to conclude that he played below his strength.

He would probably be wrong. The games in question merely exposed his deficiencies in the endgame.

The point of all this is that we should not straightjacket ourselves as being such-and-such a class of player. The "thirty-five best" table is only a guide. Don't be afraid to explore books outside your rating category. Superficial and haphazard study, however, must be avoided. We must not be afraid to review the basics, either. A single key idea that had previously escaped our attention can open up whole new worlds of understanding.

Training games using specific opening lines, unusual time limits, or the "thinking checklist" are ideal ways to focus on a specific part of the game.

Finally, (II − 31) will tell you how to train using a chess-playing computer.

STUDY COURSES

COMPLETE BEGINNERS

START WITH *A Programmed Introduction to the Game of Chess*. (If you like programmed instruction, *Bobby Fischer Teaches Chess* will provide somewhat more difficult exercises, but doesn't cover the basics as well). Next, tackle both volumes of *Learn Chess*. Volume I may prove easy after reading Sullivan's book but it contains lots of useful exercises.

Now you have more leeway in your choice of books. To start you off on the right foot, however, I recommend RHM's *Open Games*. Tarrasch proclaimed, "After the opening the gods have placed the middlegame." Znosko-Borovsky shows how to placate them with sacrifices in *The Art of Chess Combination*. Averbakh's *Essential Knowledge* is indispensable for a happy ending. These three books should form the foundation of your study. The next few, up to and including the *Dictionary of Chess*, should be used more sporadically.

The 1000 Best Short Games of Chess will dazzle and inspire you with the inexhaustible beauty and variety of chess. And the *Art of the Checkmate* will unravel the mysteries of the ever-recurring patterns which lead to mate. Both can also be enjoyed as sheer entertainment.

Logical Chess Move by Move offers insights into one of the most important and least understood aspects of chess: from start to finish every move is an indispensable link in a logical chain of events.

1001 Brilliant Ways to Checkmate and *1001 Winning Chess Sacrifices and Combinations* provide the myriad settings for familiar patterns and motifs.

The Illustrated Dictionary of Chess makes an invaluable companion for all chessplayers, but should serve especially well when you need to look up some common chess terms.

You should now go on to *The Ideas Behind the Chess Openings, The Tactics of Endgames, How to Play Chess Endings*, and *Better Chess for Average Players*. The order in which you study them is left to your discretion, *but you will want to grant them all your close attention* before turning to the program for category II players, your next step on the road to chess mastery.

NOVICES TO
CATEGORY IV (1200-1399)

This category includes players with little or no tournament experience who have also read very few chess books. More experienced players who nevertheless find themselves rated below 1400 for any considerable length of time (let's say a span of five tournaments) are in the same boat. Begin with Volume II of *Learn Chess* and thereafter follow the program suggested in the section for beginners.

CATEGORY III (1400-1599)

Look over Znosko-Borovsky's *The Art of Chess Combination* and try solving some of the positions in *1001 Winning Chess Sacrifices and Combinations*. If you can handle these with confidence, see the section for beginners on pages 24-25 and start with *The Ideas Behind the Chess Openings*. If you have trouble with these, you had best follow the advice given in the section for beginners. Start with *Open Games* and continue on from there. Keep in mind that although the program is in the section for beginners, this is a progressive course.

Also, as pointed out earlier, you may be as good as your rating indicates but still need to go back and review some basics. Lack of proficiency in just one area can stall your progress.

CATEGORY II (1600-1799)

1001 Winning Chess Sacrifices and Combinations and its companion volume provide valuable tools for players of all levels. They fit in almost anywhere, for you can use them for a few minutes or a few hours.

Again, let's begin at the beginning. Concentrate first on *Ideas Behind the Chess Openings* in order to broaden your view of the opening struggle. *A Complete Defense to 1 P-K4* and *A Complete Defense to 1 d4* will go a long way toward filling out your opening repertoire. Also consult Chapters 2, 3 and 4 of *How to Open a Chess Game*.

For more trenchant instruction, consult the brilliant *Modern Chess Opening Theory*. The Batsford and RHM books are for advanced opening preparation and expanding your repertoire. Check out the various *Chess Informants* (*The Chess Player* and *Players Chess News* as well) for the latest opening novelties.

For the endgame, give Mednis's *Practical Endgame Lessons* a try, although you may first want to review some basics with *How to Play Chess Endings*. After studying Mednis, you'll be ready to begin *Basic Chess Endings*.

Better Chess for Average Players provides a lightweight but thoughtful lead-in to more complex middlegame texts. Go on to the next section!

CATEGORY I TO
CANDIDATE MASTER (1800-2199)

The books in this section cover more complex aspects of the game, so you will need to spend more time on each one. Therefore it's even more vital to maintain a balanced program, dividing your time evenly between the opening, middlegame, and the endgame.

Modern Chess Tactics and *The Art of Attack in Chess* make ideal companion volumes. Middlegame strategy and positional play are emphasized in *Judgement and Planning in Chess* and *Modern Chess Strategy*. *Pawn Structure Chess* presents a comprehensive survey of a vital but little understood key to successful planning. *Grandmaster of Chess: Paul Keres* and *Alekhine's Best Games* contain the deepest and most instructive annotations ever written. Concentrate first on the games using the openings you play. *500 Master Games of Chess* is more lightly annotated, but spans more than a century of chess. Be selective here as well. *The Best Move* is essentially a collection of

exercises that can be used at any time. Kotov's trilogy should be studied in the order in which it's presented. *Think Like A Grandmaster*, however, deserves special attention. If you feel that your ability to calculate is poor, begin work on this book early in your program. The other two mainly rehash material covered in other books, but contain lots of challenging, thought-provoking exercises. *Grandmaster Preparation* covers various aspects of the game from the perspective of a top grandmaster. *Psychology in Chess* offers a lot of useful tips on toning up your thinking and overall approach to the game. These two books, though important, can come last.

Modern Chess Opening Theory is *the* book which explains all facets of today's sophisticated openings, and tells you how to apply and study them.

Chess Informant and the Batsford and RHM opening books should be the mainspring of your opening work. The *Encyclopedia of Chess Openings* is only for advanced players who already have fairly complete repertoires and who can make their own evaluations of opening lines.

The Batsford Endgame series and *Rook Endings* can be used mainly for adjourned games and advanced study after covering *Basic Chess Endings*.

THE THIRTY-FIVE
BEST CHESS BOOKS

1

A Programmed Introduction to the Game of Chess
Sullivan; Behavioral Research Labs

One of the few books that needs no guidelines. Visually pleasing, it offers clear and simple explanations of everything the absolute beginner needs to know in order to embark confidently on the adventure of chess. The book's real treat, however, is its continual string of graded questions about material which has just been discussed. Another strongpoint is its emphasis on certain critical aspects of the game.

2

Learn Chess: A New Way for All
Volume I - First Principles   Volume II - Winning Methods
Alexander & Beach; Pergamon

Both volumes contain exercises galore. They're a good introduction to elementary tactics, long-range planning, and typical problems of the opening, middlegame, and endgame.

The explanation of some ideas is not quite as complete as it might have been, so don't be surprised if you find yourself wondering about certain points. The exercises, too, sometimes seem a trifle difficult.

Don't try to go too fast. If you learn everything in the two books you'll have made excellent progress.

Set up the positions on your board. If you can't figure something out, make sure you've got the correct position.

When solving exercises, count material as the first step. Awareness of the material balance (generally tracked subconsciously in our games) often provides clues to the requirements of a position.

See the table on elementary calculation to help you with the exercises.

Think clearly in terms of the notation you have learned. Focus your thoughts on definite objectives. If you have difficulty with a lot of exercises, write down your thoughts and the variations you are considering. As a last resort, you can move the pieces as you're trying to solve the exercises.

3

Understanding the Open Games
Soltis, Mednis, Peters, Hartston; RHM

Simply read this one through from cover-to-cover. As you play through the games and analyses, make sure you make the moves in their proper sequence. You may find it helpful to use two boards. On one you play over the main lines, the other you use to study the variations so you don't lose track of the position. Try to figure out the next move for each side before consulting the text.

Perhaps the most important thing you can learn from this book is that *each move is based on a specific idea that fits into an overall plan conforming to the requirements of the position.*

1. At the start of the game, what is the weakest square in each player's position?
2. In the open games, development is .... and ....
3. Many open games involve the sacrifice of a pawn for a lead

in development and attacking chances. This is called a
....

4. The best way to refute a gambit is to .... it.
5. The soundest way to deal with a gambit is to ....
6. The safest way to deal with a gambit is to .... it.
7. A lead in development must be exploited by an ....,
   otherwise it will ....
8. Most play in open games takes place in the ....
   and on the ....
9. Drawish openings are often the result of ....
10. Play the openings that fit your ....

answers on p.109

4

The Art of Chess Combination
Znosko-Borovsky; Dover

Written half a century ago, some of the problems which perplexed
the author, such as classifying certain sacrifices and defining various
terms, no longer exist. They have been solved by the broader view-
point which the wealth of new experience allows. Yet Znosko-Borovsky's charming and entertaining style, fortified by his penetrating
insight into the very essence of combinative play, makes this a timeless book.

The author was one of the first to attempt the classification of
combinations based on the following criteria:

(1) Combinations based on a particular theme.

(2) Combinations based on the pieces (or sacrifices) involved.

(3) Combinations based on the type of position.

The book unravels the mysteries of the *mechanics* of combinations. It investigates how to set them up as well as how to carry
them out.

There aren't many exercises, but every position can be turned into one by covering the moves given below each diagram and attempting to work them out on your own.

This is essentially a book about *patterns*. The most critical aspects of the positions under examination recur again and again in numerous games, including yours. You will find them if you look for them.

1. What is perhaps the most important aspect of a combination? Why?
2. Give two psychological elements common to combinative play.
3. Why is the double attack so effective?
4. Combinations spring of themselves from ....

5

answers on p.109

Chess Endings: Essential Knowledge
Averbakh; Pergamon

This book definitely requires selective reading. Start with the Introduction and the brief discussion of the properties of the pieces. Then tackle the chapter on the lone King. If you have trouble corraling the King, try projecting imaginary "lines of force" along the ranks, files, and diagonals of the attacking pieces. Remember that these cast an impenetrable barrier that restrains the King. Take the Bishop and Knight mate slowly. Ignore the mate with two Knights unless it interests you.

Skip to Rook versus Knight and Rook versus Bishop. Though these two endings don't arise often, studying them will graphically demonstrate why a Rook is the more valuable piece. Study the rest of the book straight through. Later on you can come back and study

Queen against Rook. This is not only a difficult ending as it's given, but new developments indicate the inferior side can defend much more stubbornly than Averbakh indicates.

1. What is the minimum material we need to checkmate a lone King if we no longer have any Pawns?
2. What often proves to be the saving grace for the defender in Bishops-of-opposite-color endgames?
3. What characterizes the endgame?
4. What is the general method of playing a complex endgame?
5. Although we may not reach many endings in our early games, why should we begin studying the endgame now?
6. List the steps of the winning strategy for the player having an outside passed Pawn.

answers on p.109

6

The 1000 Best Short Games of Chess
Fireside; Chernev

Take a few games at a time or as many as you can handle. Try to guess the moves before you look at the text. Look for themes such as the fork, pin, etc., and for typical mating patterns.

7

The Art of the Checkmate
Renaud and Kahn; Dover

The most important patterns for inexperienced players to learn are mates. This little gem of a book outlines and explains the most common mates. It presents them in numerous schematic diagrams highlighting their outstanding features, and analyzes lively games in which the various mating ideas played a key role. Quizzes every few chapters allow you to practice finding and executing the mates yourself. See the section on *1001 Brilliant Ways to Checkmate* for suggestions on working out exercises.

Logical Chess Move by Move
Chernev; Fireside

An opportunity to observe how masters think and apply general principles. Chernev's sense of humor, spritely prose and pointed explanations of underlying ideas are only part of this book's charm. A varied selection of games introduce the reader to a host of plans and motifs linked by notes following *every* move.

1. According to Tarrasch, what is the strongest attacking piece? (pg.10)
2. After 1 e4 e5 2 Nf3 Nc6 3 Bc4 Bc5 4 c3 Qe7 5 0-0 d6 6 d4, is 6...exd4 a reasonable move? (pg.13)
3. Is Black's plan in game two contrary to the demands of the position? Why, or why not?

4. How should one best oppose a kingside attack? (pg.23)
5. Why is 4...exf4 a bad move following 1 e4 e5 2 f4 Bc5 3 Nc3 Nc6 4 Nf3? (pg.28)
6. What is the key move in the Colle? (pg.46)
7. What's wrong with 6 Nxd5, after 1 d4 d5 2 c4 e6 3 Nc3 Nf6 4 Bg5 Nbd7 5 cxd5 exd5? (pg.202)
8. How does Black equalize in QP openings? (pg.220)
9. What file is generally opened first for White in the Queen's Gambit Declined?

answers on p.109

9

1001 Brilliant Ways to Checkmate
1001 Winning Chess Sacrifices and Combinations
Reinfeld; Wilshire Book Company

Two thousand-and-two exercises for the inexperienced. Remember patterns, look for specific themes to employ, think in terms of specific moves and countermoves. Try to isolate the few (or only) revelant moves available on each turn ("candidate moves") in order to narrow the scope of the variations you must consider. See the review tables on "Thinking" and "Elementary Calculation". Also see (12; and, for more advanced thinking techniques, 33).

10

An Illustrated Dictionary of Chess
Brace; McKay

A useful reference work for all players, but especially valuable for those needing to look up terms they are just learning.

11

The Ideas behind the Chess Openings
Fine; McKay

One of the best stylists in chess, Fine has written a comprehensive survey that has never been equalled. Some specific lines are out of date, but the opening ideas are timeless. Probably the first work making extensive use of diagrams contrasting pawn skeletons with full-board positions.

Careful study of pages 1–9, 102–109, and 158–160 will repay handsome dividends.

Although a thorough grasp of the overall opening struggle is essential, it is impossible to know and play well more than a small fraction of opening theory. You should therefore concentrate on those lines fitting your repertoire, or on closely related variations that will broaden your perspective on various middlegame schemes. (The evaluations of the chances offered by the French Defense pawn structures in diagrams 13A–13E can be very misleading.)

A good way to select an opening repertoire is to gather together the games of a player you would like to emulate (your styles must jibe) and play the same openings he plays. For further advice on selecting and perfecting openings, see (15, 34; also II-2, 3, and 7.)

Match the names of the *openings* (listed below) with their *key moves* and *characteristics* (listed on the next page.)

a.	ENGLISH	k.	MODERN BENONI
b.	CATALAN	l.	EVANS GAMBIT
c.	PONZIANI	m.	NIMZO-INDIAN
d.	KING'S INDIAN	n.	SCOTCH GAME
e.	DUTCH	o.	KGA
f.	CENTER COUNTER	p.	SLAV
g.	QGA	q.	EXCHANGE RUY LOPEZ
h.	CARO-KANN	r.	FRENCH
i.	BUDAPEST	s.	TWO KNIGHTS
j.	QUEEN'S INDIAN	t.	SICILIAN

1.	1 e4 e5 2 f4 exf4	A. Trappy defense to 1 d4.
2.	1 d4 Nf6 2 c4 e6 3 Nc3	B. Most dynamic counter to 1 e4.
	Bb4	C. Fighting defense to 1 d4.
3.	1 e4 e5 2 Nf3 Nc6	D. Antiquated opening lacking punch.
	3 Bc4 Bc5 4 b4	E. Ambitious kingside designs.
4.	1 e4 e6 2 d4 d5	F. Risky offshoot of Giuoco Piano.
5.	1 e4 e5 2 Nf3 Nc6	G. Active alternative for Black to 1 d4 d5.
	3 Bb5 a6 4 Bxc6	H. Swashbuckling gambit.
6.	1 d4 d5 2 c4 c6	I. Uncomplicated piece play.
7.	1 c4	J. Alternative for Black to Giuoco Piano.
8.	1 e4 e5 2 Nf3 Nc6 3 c3	K. Heads straight for the endgame.
9.	1 d4 d5 2 c4 e6	L. Positional offshoot of Queen's Gambit.
	3 Nf3 Nf6 4 g3	M. Flexible White hypermodern strategy.
10.	1 e4 c5	N. Open play versus 1 d4.
11.	1 d4 f5	O. Theoretically doubtful reply to 1 e4.
12.	1 e4 c6 2 d4 d5	P. Cramped, unbalanced, strategic play.
13.	1 e4 d5	Q. Solid, passive defense to 1 e4.
14.	1 d4 Nf6 2 c4 c5 3 d5	R. Cousin to Caro-Kann.
15.	1 d4 d5 2 c4 dxc4	S. Razor-sharp counter to 1 d4.
16.	1 d4 Nf6 2 c4 e5	T. Sister to Nimzo-Indian.
17.	1 d4 Nf6 2 c4 e6	
	3 Nf3 b6	
18.	1 d4 Nf6 2 c4 g6	
	3 Nc3 Bg7 4 e4	
19.	1 e4 e5 2 Nf3 Nc6	
	3 Bc4 Nf6	
20.	1 e4 e5 2 Nf3 Nc6	
	3 d4 cxd4 4 Nxd4	

answers on p.109

40

12

Better Chess for Average Players
Harding; Oxford University Press

A better-than-average book. In fact, the best ever written for promoting real comprehension and developing the playing skills of the average player. Follow the chessic misadventures of Harry Hacker and Johnny Brain through thirty units of instruction covering everything from the basic material values to over-the-board analysis of complicated positions.

13

The Tactics of Endgames
Ban; Branden Press

Over two hundred piquant studies in which art imitates chess lend credence to the author's contention that tactical motifs stand out best against the background of simple endgames. Carefully chosen for their artistic merit as well as their instructional value, these studies will prove challenging, indeed. See the section on *1001 Brilliant Ways to Checkmate* for advice on solving exercises.

14

How to Play Chess Endings
Znosko-Borovsky; Dover

Containing a wealth of instruction, this book is a delight to read. The next step up the endgame ladder from *Essential Knowledge*. Read it right through to the end. You'll probably have trouble putting it down. See also (I - 2, 18, 19).

1. What are three common drawing devices in the endgame?
2. In this phase of the game, both the .... and the
   .... experience a great ....of roles compared to the opening or middlegame.
3. What is the central focus of endgame play?
4. The .... Pawn is exceptional, due to the geometrical limitations of the chessboard.
5. What piece is ideally suited to the endgame?
6. A Bishop hemmed in by its own Pawns is a .... Bishop.
7. Contrast the Bishop and the Knight.
8. White's King is on g3, Black's on c4. White has Pawns on a2 and c2. What's the result?
9. Passed Pawns are special. What is the most special type of passed Pawn?

answers on p.110

15

How to Open a Chess Game
Evans, Gligoric, Hort, Petrosian, Keres, Larsen, Portisch; RHM

Chapters one and two are rather elementary. Each succeeding chapter covers a specific aspect of the openings as seen through the eyes of a top-ranked grandmaster. Chapter four, "Developing an Opening Repertoire," addresses most directly the questions likely to be posed by the average player. Chapter seven, "The Secret Workshop of a Grandmaster," by Keres, is perhaps the most revealing. (For examples of meticulously worked out openings or repertoires, See 18 and 34; I - 5 and 6).

16

Practical Endgame Lessons
Mednis; McKay

A thoughtful survey of the *practical* difficulties involved in winning won endgames, or drawing inferior ones, and how they may be overcome. Fills the gap between *How to Play Chess Endings* and *Basic Chess Endings*. (See I - 2, 18, 19).

17

Judgment and Planning in Chess
Euwe; McKay

Clear, methodical and profound. This book will teach you:
* How to draw up and carry out plans conforming to the requirements of a position.
* How the opening influences the middlegame.
* How the opening books reach their conclusions.
* How to evaluate positions by weighing their outstanding positional features.
* How to support or verify your evaluations with deep analysis.
* Some standard middlegame plans in the most popular openings.

Profound, original strategists can be seen at work in (I - 12, 13, and 17). (II - 16, 17, and 18 provide numerous examples of the increasingly sophisticated handling of thematic middlegames over the course of a century.

More experienced players may want to use this book in order to review specific middlegame ideas, but those unfamiliar with the concept of detailed planning should work through the entire book.

1. How does positional understanding grow?
2. The viability of a whole set of variations, especially in the opening, often depends on the assessment of a single ....
   ....
3. What important psychological principle must we bear in mind once we gain a comfortable material advantage?
4. Different kinds of positions require different methods of analysis and evaluation. Elaborate a few of them.

5. What is perhaps the most important consideration when evaluating *any* position?
6. State two advantages of a queenside pawn majority.
7. Even if we don't exploit a positional advantage directly, its .... often causes the opponent to further compromise his position.
8. What does the transition from the position in diagram nineteen to that in diagram twenty teach us?
9. From the defender's point of view, the creation of a .... is nearly always fatal.
10. Convert .... enduring advantages into .... enduring ones.
11. Pawn advances must be .... Why?
12. What is the central point of the discussion on page twenty-three?

answers on p.110

18

A Complete Defense to 1 P-K4
A Complete Defense to 1 d4
Cafferty and Hooper; Pergamon

These companion volumes provide the basis for developing a working repertoire against White's two most popular opening moves. Besides being complete, they are ideal for players with limited time at their disposal for opening study. The openings in question lead to middlegames whose underlying ideas are relatively easy to comprehend, and which offer scope for creative, wide-open piece play. A carefully thought out repertoire will enable you to begin every game with confidence.

Refer to "Study Hints" for suggestions on learning variations. Be sure you understand the reasoning behind the evaluations of the various lines (for clarification, see *Judgment and Planning in Chess*). Don't be afraid to question the evaluations if you feel there is a valid reason for doing so. Trace the effects of the openings throughout the course of the representative games appended to each chapter. Refer to *"Chess Informant"*, the *"Chess Player"*, and the *"Players Chess News"* for the latest games in your openings.

A detailed discussion of the isolated QP positions characterizing the Queen's Gambit Accepted can be found in *Modern Chess Strategy*.

1. What is the spirit of Petroff's Defense?
2. Why is it difficult for White to maintain the initiative against it?
3. In Petroff's Defense, if White delays castling, why is it generally a good idea for Black to do so as well?
4. What is White's main break in the Queen's Gambit Accepted?
5. Why is it usually so effective in securing White an advantage?
6. What is the danger of an early development of the Black Queen's Bishop in many double QP openings?
7. What are the pluses and minuses of the move a4 for White in the QGA?
8. What is the critical position of the Modern Variation?
9. In the main line, what is the chief difference between the moves 4 Nf3 and 4 Nc3?
10. When studying closely related opening lines, we should pay special attention to .... and .... — ....

answers on p.110

19

Modern Chess Tactics:
Volume I - Pieces and Pawns In Action
Volume II - Attack and Defense
Pachman; McKay

Approach each position as an exercise, and keep track of the time it takes to solve each one. Over the course of time you'll be able to see which types of positions and motifs give you the most trouble. You may want to write down your analysis right after you've made it, then compare it to the lines in the book. Note questions that remain unanswered so you can return to them later.

On the whole, these books are excellent. They entertain as well as instruct. You will, however, find a number of positions in which playable alternatives escaped the author's attention. (In Volume I, Diagram 18, for example, is 1...hxg5 2 Nd6† Kd7 3 Nxf7 Qe8 4 Nxh8 Kc7 really so horrible for Black? And what about his chances of survival after 1...dxe4!?! 2 Bxf7† Kxf7 3 Qxd8 hxg5? In any event, both of these lines are better for Black than the one he actually played. Errors of this sort are practically unavoidable in a work of this scope, so we should not judge the author harshly.)(See 21; I - 4, 5, 8, 9, 20, 21, 23 and 24; II - 13, 14, 19, 20 and 21).

1. Failure to recognize the .... in the game can result in a loss of the .... and a .... alteration in the course of the game.
2. Excessive .... in the opponent's .... is a common psychological error in tactical play.
3. The .... in which moves are played often determines

the success or failure of a combination.

4. Moves can be ...., ..., or ....

5. .... of the pieces multiplies their ....

answers on p.111

20

Modern Chess Strategy
Pachman; Dover

The natural complement to Modern Chess Tactics, it is no less methodical, complete and instructive. Sit back and relax as the author effortlessly guides you from the most basic considerations of chess strategy to the most complex. (See I - 1, 2, 3, 4, 5, 12, 13, 15, 17, 22 and 25; II - 8, 9 and 11).

1. What are the two faces of the equilibrium?
2. What else must be done after hitting upon a plan?
3. Explain good and bad Bishops.
4. Opposite-colored Bishops represent a strong drawing factor in the endgame. How does their presence influence the middle-game?
5. Which piece can remain poorly placed for a long time?
6. How are the Rooks most often brought into play? Why?
7. The heavy pieces are ill-suited for ....
8. Which piece loves a blockade?
9. What are some general considerations of isolated QP middle-games?
10. Why are two weaknesses so often fatal?
11. Why do we need to attain a certain degree of central control before attempting to post a piece there?
12. The success of an attack depends on an initial ....

answers on p.111

21

The Art of Attack in Chess
Vukovic; Pergamon

A brilliant survey of every aspect of the attack on the King. Vukovic's main interest is the discovery of the ultimate truths about such attacks. When should they be launched? What are the risks involved? What are the indicators of success? What does the future of chess portend for the attacking style?

Vukovic analyses the elements of attacks on the King singly and in concert, from every possible vantage point. He examines the effects of each piece, the creation and use of open lines, cooperation between the pieces and the pawns, the discoveries of the great attacking players, etc., etc. (See I - 4, 7, 10, 14, 20, 21, 23 and 24; II - 19 and 20).

1. .... is the basis of a game of chess.
2. What is the chief obstacle that causes many masters to shy away from an attacking style?
3. The attack against the uncastled King in the opening frequently occurs .... the ....
4. The .... is the most common tactical device employed in this attack.
5. What is the chief principle in the attack on the King?
6. When pursuing the King, we should refrain from checking him at random, but select the .... and .... — ....
7. Castled positions are, as a rule, ... formations.
8. The pieces should concentrate their attacking powers on .... — ....

9. What should we guard against when setting in motion a pawn avalanche against the enemy King?

answers on p.111

22

Pawn Structure Chess
Soltis; McKay

In contrast to the highly mobile pieces, the overall pawn formation changes rather slowly. Since the pawn structure defines the open lines and outposts used by the pieces, familiarity with the potential changes inherent in related structures - called families - is essential to forming a carrying out productive long-range plans.

Soltis examines the pros and cons of each principal type of pawn structure by tracing the evolution and effects of each through numerous illustrative games. He rounds out each sub-section of the book with supplemental games illustrating further nuances in pawn play.

This is a book that every player should read from start to finish, even though each chapter is really an independent guide to the most common middlegame plans arising in certain major openings. (See 20 and II - 9 for more about the strategic handling of the Pawns).

1. What are a few major characteristics of the Caro-Slav formation?
2. What central square must White try to dominate in the open Sicilian structure?
3. Black's main trump in this formation is his ....
   ....
4. Pawn chains that cross the central dividing line exert a ....
   ....
5. The natural way to attack a pawn chain is at ....
6. Why?

7. Why should we think in terms of structures rather than openings?
8. What are three common pawn formations, or plans, in double QP openings?
9. One defensive idea for Black against the minority attack is to set up a blockade on the square ....

answers on p.112

23

Grandmaster of Chess: The Complete Games of Paul Keres
Keres; Arco

A far from complete collection of magnificent games spanning a generation of chess. The depth and clarity of Keres's annotations are the highlight of this book. They reveal how one of the greatest players of all time successfully put into practice the myriad ideas collectively known as chess theory. The games sparkle with energy and imagination, and the roster of Keres's victims reads like a "who's who" of chess. Keres was a true virtuoso who could handle any type of position superbly, so this book contains something for everyone, regardless of their playing style. Middle-range category II players and below should read the book straight through, while stronger players, if they don't mind missing a real treat, can concentrate on games employing their favorite openings.

24

500 Master Games of Chess
Tartakover and DuMont; Dover

The more than six hundred and fifty pages of this massive tome overflow with a diversity of the best chess played over a period of more than one hundred and fifty years. It's hard to say what you'll enjoy most about this book. The thoughtfully chosen games are unsurpassed in beauty, originality, profundity and instruction, but so are the pithy notes and introductions to each one. Whether you study the games at random, or select them on the basis of openings or middlegames, you will find both enjoyment and instruction galore (and greatly increase your vocabulary as well).

25

Modern Chess Opening Theory
Suetin; Pergamon

Absolutely the best general treatise ever written on the openings. The author, a strong Soviet grandmaster still active on the international circuit, omits nothing. The book's only flaw is that it has not been revised since its publication in 1954, and some of Suetin's evaluations of popular lines have since been overturned. This is especially obvious when we open to page 190 and read his conclusions on the 6 Bg5 line in the Najdorf Sicilian. This flaw has a positive side, however. It points up the difficulty of evaluating a complex opening system without the benefit of a broad database of grandmaster games, and it reveals the richness of chess. (See I - 4, 5, 6, 8, and 15 for players with highly refined opening play. Also see II - 7).

1. What is perhaps the most important aim of the opening?
2. What is the classical method of central control? The hypermodern?
3. Pressure .... the .... squares may be more effective than .... them.
4. Give two reasons why controlling the center is important.
5. Although each position may be influenced by general principles, a .... to solving its problems is essential.
6. We must consider the .... as well as the .... features of a position.
7. In fact, in many of today's openings, Black's battle cry is "......................!"
8. The opening struggle may assume a .... character in which the main clash is deferred to the middlegame, or .... variations may arise during the first few moves.
9. The spirit of counterattack allows for the creation of .... that are offset by .... piece play.
10. One cannot study the opening properly without giving due attention to ....
11. Modern openings aim at leaving the player with a .... to pursue in the ....
12. Why do modern masters shy away from most double KP openings in favor of the Ruy Lopez?
13. A pawn center can be very strong, if .... and ....
14. The positional superiority that led to Botvinnik's famous win over Capablanca at the A.V.R.O. Tournament in 1938 was a ....
15. Many modern openings are struggles for the ....

16. Suetin's overall approach to understanding the opening is to
    .... the different forms of the struggle.

answers on p.112

26

Chess Informant

A series published twice a year in Yugoslavia by the same folks who created the *Encyclopedia of Chess Openings*. Each volume contains approximately six hundred annotated games from the previous six-month period. The games are selected first on the basis of their theoretical importance, then on their general interest, though all are of relatively high quality. The latest issue, number 31, covers games from the first half of 1981.

The games are origanized by a unique and efficient coding system which, however, does not jibe with the one used in the *Encyclopedia*. Later issues of *Chess Informant* also include the *Encyclopedia* code for each game. *Chess Informant*'s timeliness and organization make it the ideal tool for keeping up with the latest novelties in your favorite openings.

It contains crosstables of the major tournaments, and a tabulated vote by the editors on the "ten best games" and "ten most important novelties" of the previous issue. There is also a varied selection of middlegames and endgames that didn't make it into the main body of the book.

Despite all these assets, *Chess Informant* has a serious flaw. Many of the notes to the games are hastily written and contain numerous mistakes. Trust only the annotations of Timman, Karpov, Hubner and a few other top-ranked players. In the end, however, you should rely on your own judgment. (See II - 31).

27

Batsford, RHM Opening Series

These books examine a single opening (Batsford's *Modern Defense*) or system (RHM's *Najdorf Variation*). Covering each book would be impossible, so my intention here is to introduce them to readers who are unfamiliar with this kind of opening text.

They represent the middle ground between books like *The Ideas Behind the Chess Openings* and the *Encyclopedia of Chess Openings*. They offer hints on the correct handling of the opening in question as well as in-depth analysis. Other publishers besides Batsford and RHM also print this type of opening book, but only these two offer a fairly extensive line of consistently high-quality books. The Batsford series covers more openings, but their books are much more expensive than RHM's.

For hints on studying the openings and building a repertoire, (see 11, 15, 25, 33, and 34; II - 1, 2, 3, 4, 5, 6, 7, and 10).

28

Basic Chess Endings
Fine; McKay

Before the appearance of the Batsford endgame series in the mid-seventies, Fine's prodigious book, first published in 1941, was the standard English language reference work on the endgame. Despite various analytical errors (see I I - 23), it remains a great book. It's still the only single-volume work of its kind in English, and, given today's rapidly rising book prices, that's an important point. The general methods of handling endgames have been covered (rather more interestingly) in (14), while (16) contains a wealth of practical advice. The main value of this book for us lies in its comprehensive scope. It encompasses every common ending likely to arise in our games.

If you take your endgames seriously, you'll probably want to follow the advice on studying the endgame given in "Study Hints" (pg. 13). (See I - 2, 4, 5, 7, 8, 9, 13 and 18. Also 34 and II - 10 and 22).

The most important endgames: For the sake of completeness, we include those endings already encountered in some of the other books we recommend. If you prefer, you can just go over the main lines. Skip the examples marked "a", "b", etc. Once you study a number of endgames, you will be better able to decide what proportion of those listed here you can handle over a particular period of time.

King and Pawn Endgames
850, 60, 63, 64, 68, 69, 77, 85, 88, 91.
Knight Endgames
102, 107, 108, 112, 115, 122, 125-128, 130, 132, 134, 138.
Bishop Endgames
142, 144, 158, 168, 170-176, 182, 183, 184, 186, 191, 193, 200-206, 210, 214.
Bishop vs. Knight Endgames
216-222, 225, 231, 232, 233, 236, 237, 241, 251, 257, 267, 269.
Rook Endgames
281, 285, 286, 291, 292, 296, 297, 301, 303-305, 307, 309, 312, 319, 323, 326, 332, 341, 344, 347, 352, 360, 367, 368, 369, 370, 375, 377, 382, 386,393, 400, 404, 414, 422, 425, 434.

Rook vs. Minor Piece Endgames
442, 453, 454, 458, 460-467, 471, 472, 480, 489, 496-506, 509, 516, 518, 523-528, 536-539.

Queen Endgames
544-556, 560, 562, 565, 566, 567, 571, 579, 581, 589, 594, 595, 597-603.

The theory of some Queen and Pawn vs. Queen endgames is still in a state of flux. The endgame Queen vs. Rook is not as easy to win as it seems. Hidden resources have recently been found for the defender.

1. King and Pawn endgames are ....
2. What are some typical ideas arising in King and Pawn endings?
3. Knights cannot .... a ....
4. Beware of a Bishop and RP ....
5. Knights have great trouble stopping ....
6. Keep your Pawns .... the .... squares as your Bishop.
7. An active Rook is often worth ....
8. Rook endgames introduce the drawing device of ....
   ....
9. The passed Pawn is especially terrifying in ....
   ....
10. When defending, trade ....
11. Avoid unjustified .... advances.
12. When ahead in material, ...
13. When ahead in material, don't ....

answers on p.112

29

Batsford Endgame Series;
Rook Endings

These books cover the same material as *Basic Chess Endings*, but in somewhat greater detail. They are for the serious tournament player who wants to have the very best and most complete material available for adjournment analysis. They also contain lucid instruction on how to play the various endgames, but obtaining the entire collection will prove to be a substantial financial investment for the average player. (See 14, 16, 28; II - 22).

30

My Best Games of Chess
1908-1923; 1924-1937
Alekhine; McKay

Dr. Alexander Alexandrovich Alekhine, in terms of his games, results, writings, and passion for chess, was the greatest player who ever lived. The man who dethroned the legendary Capablanca in 1927 has left a legacy of games whose power, grace, subtlety and imagination will leave the reader dumbfounded. His constant striving for the initiative from the very first move has become the hallmark of the supergrandmasters. His ability (and desire) to explain the motivations behind his moves makes this collection of games an invaluable addition to the serious player's arsenal.

We also highly recommend *The Book of the New York Interna-*

tional Chess Tournament, 1924. Dr. Alekhine has deeply annotated every game of this classic event, which brought together just about every great player of that time — including Lasker, Capablanca, and Reti.

31

The Best Move
Hort and Jansa; RHM

Two hundred and thirty positions, many taken from the authors' own games, challenge you in a number of ways. In most cases you must assess the position and support your evaluation with at least one variation. Others may ask you to find the best move, or a host of variations. Points are awarded for the various moves so that you can grade your results at the end.

32

Psychology in Chess
Krogius; RHM

The Soviets currently lead the world in "para-psychological research," and as anyone who followed the antics surrounding the 1978 world championship match could tell you, they are putting this research to work in the field of chess. The author is a Soviet grandmaster and psychologist who assisted Boris Spassky in his 1972 world title bout with Bobby Fischer. Although he avoids discussing esoteric topics such as hypnotism and mind control, he does probe quite deeply into the possible sources of the common errors that plague even grandmasters. Many of psychology's observations about chess are still very speculative, but this book contains much food for thought for the practical player.

33

Think Like a Grandmaster
Play Like a Grandmaster
Train Like a Grandmaster
Kotov; Batsford

Think Like a Grandmaster is one of the best-selling chess books ever written. This is really no surprise, as it is the only book investigating the practical player's thought processes in detail. It is crammed with instruction on study, planning, positional play and chessboard psychology. Numerous exercises that closely simulate the requirements of over-the-board play provide an added treat.

The other two books in this series are somewhat disappointing, though they do contain enough practical advice and exercises to make worthwhile reading. (See **34**; II - 10, 23).

1. Describe the steps in a grandmaster's thought processes.
2. Unless we have ample time in a critical situation, we should .... variations ....
3. We should not consider .... moves, nor ....

4. Is the analysis of the position in diagram 3 (Flohr-Fine, Hastings 1935/36) correct?
5. What are the three keys to successful thinking in chess?

6. The extent of our analysis depends on whether there are
   .... or .... variations.
7. We should first consider ...., ... moves.
8. What is a candidate move?
9. Overlooking even a .... can be fatal.
10. Beware of the ....
11. A frequent source of errors is the ....
12. What types of plans are there?
13. What is the best home-study tool?
14. The .... use of .... is a pre-
    requisite of over-the-board success.
15. Advanced players will make rapid progress if they ....
    their own games .... and ....

answers on p.113

34

Grandmaster Preparation
Polugayevsky; Pergamon

One of the world's top ten players, who narrowly missed becoming this year's world championship challenger, bares his soul while fulfilling his obligation to the chess public.

The book contains three distinct parts. The first is a detailed account of the author's trials, tribulations and triumphs with the opening variation of the Sicilian Defense that bears his name. The second is the most revealing and instructive material ever written concerning the analysis of adjourned games. Part three contains level-headed advice for dealing with the pressures of intense tournament situations.

This book will show you how opening theory evolves, and the depth to which today's opening connoisseurs prepare for each game. It emphasizes once again the need for specialization, and the way in which it helped the author to scale the heights in chess. You will also learn a lot about the Sicilian Defense itself. (See 25; II - 10, 22).

1. What are some general considerations in the analysis of adjourned games?
2. Our motto when deciding which opening to play in important games should be, "........................".
3. Perhaps the most important factor in analysis and over-the-board play is ....

35

answers on p.113

Encyclopedia of Chess Openings
Volumes I - V (A - E)

A comprehensive survey of current chess theory. Written by strong, active grandmasters, many of whom specialize in the openings they analyze here, these books are indispensable for the serious tournament player.

Except for the names of players, tournaments, annotators, and a brief explanation of the symbols employed, they contain not a single word of text. Instead you'll find in row after row of chess moves, the interrelated main lines of an opening. These are supplemented by numerous footnotes offering alternative continuations. Each line of analysis is followed by a symbol evaluating the chances.

The books contain little independent analysis. Just about every line has been taken from an actual game. This is understandable in view of the extremely competitive nature of tournament chess — grandmasters want to keep their opening ideas to themselves until they have a chance to spring them on unsuspecting opponents.

Locating the analysis of a line you're interested in takes some doing if you're not familiar with the layout of each book. Volume I, designated ("C"), contains the French Defense, Ruy Lopez, and other double KP openings. Volume II ("B") deals with all the other KP openings, such as the Sicilian, Caro-Kann, etc.; III ("D") analyses the double QP openings and the Gruenfeld; IV ("E") contains the King's Indian, Nimzo-Indian, and related lines; and V ("A") covers the Dutch, Modern Benoni, Benko Gambit, English, etc.

Let's take a look at Volume IV ("E") to see how we'd look up a particular line. The main openings, or divisions of each opening, are given along with their code numbers boxed in red on pages 8 and 9. Thus if we were interested in the Saemisch variation of the King's Indian, we would find, on page 9, the moves 1 d4 Nf6 2 c4 g6 3 Nc3 Bg7 4 e4 d6 5 f3 preceded by the number 370, which indicates a page, and followed by E8. Turning to page 370, we find that the Saemisch is subdivided into ten sections, from E80 to E89. In order to avoid wasting time flipping back and forth through the book every time you want to look something up, keep track of the letter-number code of the line you're interested in, and look in the book for that code rather than the page number. Many publications containing current games include the *Encyclopedia* code along with the game.

A note of warning. These books are remarkably free of typographic errors, but the evaluations of the lines do not include a money-back guarantee. Think for yourself, and use these books as guidelines only.

REVIEW TABLES

The review tables presented in this chapter are unique in both layout and intent. Each table, which can be used in various ways, outlines the principal ideas and playing techniques pertaining to certain aspects of the game, such as strategy, the opening, and so on.

By reviewing the tables before a tournament or game, the ideas will be fresh in your mind, and this will help you hit upon the "right idea at the right time". After a game, they can help you pinpoint and eliminate weaknesses in your play by offering clues to the correct procedure in those instances where you went astray. By refering to the tables during practice games, either throughout the games or at previously specified intervals, you will develop good thinking habits and broaden the spectrum of statagems at your command under normal tournament conditions.

Versatility was also the watchword in setting out the series of diagrams at the end of this chapter. Compare the representative positions and their respective strategies with those occurring in your own games. By doing this soon after you finish playing, when everything is still vivid in your mind, you will reduce the number of future occasions on which you "zig" when you should "zag".

The diagrams have been laid out to enhance their visual effect and to allow ready comparison of related positions. Use them as a set of exercises as well. Elucidate the main features and motifs of each position, then turn to the continuations given at the back of this book.

The Pawns

Pawns are plodding and humble, the luckless peasants of the chessboard. Best suited for defense, the thankless task of shielding the King falls upon their heads. They're called on to prop up Knights and bolster Bishops; Rooks, too, sometimes enlist their support. The Pawn's every move leaves a weakness in its train. When they step out of line, or become separated from their fellows, they fall prey to marauders or chafe beneath the bootheels of blockaders. When deployed in attack, they are ruthlessly exchanged or mercilessly sacrificed to create inroads for the pieces. Pawns are tenacious; they stake out territory and cling to it doggedly. Their hour of glory arrives when they queen.

Despite their miserable lot, the Pawns find strength in numbers, and have the greatest say when battle plans are drawn.

The Knight

Knights are special, and they know it. It matters little to them that Bishops, Rooks, and Queens can glide gracefully over the board; that Kings move with regal grace and deliberation; that the Pawns shuffle forward, each setting his own pace, toward a glorious destiny. For only Knights can defy the law of gravity and leap over any obstacle. The rest of the chessboard's populace, squarebound, can only stand and gape at his antics as they trod on one another's toes.

The Knight's unique power makes him a show-off. He loves center stage, where he can radiate his influence in all directions. He dreads being banished to the wings; he loathes languishing in corners. A vague sense of inferiority haunts him, though, because he can't get around quickly. His insecurity manifests in a chronic need for the support of the other men, especially the Pawns, and in a desire to operate from safe havens.

Extremely chivalrous, the Knight never shirks his duty. Tactically, he shows a flair for forks; his strategic specialty is blockading Pawns. His sovereign always rests easy when he's near at hand. The Knight is curiously inept, however, at shepherding passed Pawns.

The Bishop

Bishops spread the gospel best on long open diagonals. Working in unison seems to invest them with a supernatural power, for their strength more than doubles. Alone, however, they can be feeble indeed, for even the most zealous cleric must confine his preaching to half the kingdom. The Bishop's knack for looking after passed Pawns from afar is a strong endgame asset. Fianchettoed Bishops often perform the dual functions of raining fire and brimstone on the enemy while offering their own King protective benedictions.

The Rook

Rooks are haughty, independent creatures. Proud of their strength, they can easily mate a lone King; delivering perpetual check at a distance is child's play for them. To avoid harassment, they stand aloof as their inferiors skirmish in the center. This curtails their power not a whit, however. Open files are their domain. On penetrating to the seventh rank, Rooks exult; they terrify the hostile Pawns. Reaching the eighth rank, their quarry is the King. Supporting passed Pawns, their effect is that of tightly coiled springs. Although they are capable enough in defense, a passive Rook is a sorry sight.

The Queen

Her majesty is truly the power behind the throne: no corner of the kingdom lies beyond her reach. Kings venture forth at their peril when she roams the board. Her mere presence frequently heralds a mating attack. Her high station forbids hand-to-hand fighting, however. Excelling in lightning raids, the Queen is a nonpareil of versatility.

The King

Victim of relentless persecution, the King cowers in the corner for most of the game. Only in the endgame can he redeem himself. No longer fearing for his life, his mettle matches that of the Bishop or the Knight. Here he extracts his revenge by wreaking havoc on the lead-footed enemy Pawns. The King makes amends to his foot-soldiers for his earlier cowardice by providing them with a safe escort to the eighth rank.

STRATEGY
"Coordination is the key"

— *SEIZE space.*
— *PROVOKE, ENTICE, or FORCE your opponent to weaken Pawns and squares.*
— *INFILTRATE weak square complexes.*
— *RESTRAIN first, then BLOCKADE, and ultimately DESTROY your opponent's weak Pawns.*
— *PROTECT or ELIMINATE weaknesses.*
— *REINFORCE and OCCUPY outposts.*
— *CENTRALIZE the pieces.*
— *DOMINATE open lines.*
— *REDEPLOY pieces to HEIGHTEN their activity and ENHANCE their coordination.*
— *ADVANCE mobile majorities.*
— *BLOCKADE passed Pawns.*
— *ATTACK the King.*

— *CAPTURE material.*
— *EXCHANGE or DRIVE OFF the opponent's active pieces.*
— *WIN tempi.*
— *SIMPLIFY into superior endgames.*
— *PLACE your opponent in zugzwang.*
— *WAIT for your opponent to declare his intentions.*
— *MANEUVER.*
— *DELIVER perpetual check.*
— *SECURE a stalemate.*
— *OBTAIN the opposition.*
— *TRIANGULATE.*
— *PLAY for the two Bishops.*
— *REMAIN with the superior minor piece.*
— *GO for the good Bishop.*
— *MAINTAIN options.*
— *CONVERT advantages.*
— *COUNTERATTACK.*
— *ATTACK weaknesses on both sides of the board alternately.*
— *WREST the initiative.*
— *EXPLOIT errors.*
— *DEFUSE threats.*
— *CALCULATE variations.*
— *VISUALIZE and EVALUATE positions.*
— *EXECUTE sacrifices and combinations.*
— *DEFEND coolly, stubbornly, and resourcefully.*
— *ATTACK relentlessly and ingeniously.*
— *COMPLICATE deliberately.*
— *PINPOINT crisis points.*
— *MAKE moves in the proper order.*
— *TRANSPOSE into favorable positions.*
— *CONTROL the center.*
— *DEVELOP all the pieces.*

- *SEQUESTER the king.*
- *ACTIVATE the King in the endgame.*
- *FREE cramped positions through exchanges.*
- *BREAK attacks by RETURNING material.*
- *SET traps.*

TACTICS
"Combinations are the heart of chess".

— *Alekhine*

- Tactical coordination of the pieces multiplies their strength.
- Zero in on focal-points.
- Force your opponent's replies.
- Create more than one threat at a time.
- Checkmate, win material, attain a positional advantage, equalize, or reduce your inferiority by employing the following devices:

Pinning	*Trapping*	*Clearance*
Forking	*Diverting*	*Interference*
Skewering	*Decoying*	*The Desperado*
Discovered attack	*The Zwischenzug*	*The Back-Rank Mate*
Double attack	*Surprise moves*	
Double check	*Quiet moves*	

THINKING

- *Keep track of material at all times.*
- *Never give away even a single pawn without good reason.*
- *Outline specific plans and goals.*
- *Formulate them in your mind clearly and completely.*
- *Filter out irrelevant moves. Concentrate on "candidates."*

During a game you just don't have the time to ask yourself all of the following questions after each one of your opponent's moves. Fortunately, it's not necessary to do so, else the game would become a tedious chore. The secret of their successful application is selectivity. Once you have asked most of these questions, the answers you come up with will carry over to the next few moves. There is no set order in which to ask them — it all depends on the position.

Some you simply MUST ask after every move your opponent makes (unless you've already taken the move into account and prepared a reply). After a little practice, however, you will find yourself seeking the answers to these questions without actually formulating them.

1.   *What new and immediate one-move threats has my opponent's last move created? How can I answer it?*
2.   *Has the move created any other immediate threats? (Those of more than one move). How can I parry it?*
3.   *What threats can I set up? How?*
4.   *Have I seen this position, or a similar one before?*
5.   *If so: who stands better, and what is the best plan for carrying it out?*
6.   *If not: What are the outstanding features and elements of this position, and what plan(s) and method(s) of achieving it are available?*
7.   *Who stands better in this position? Why? How much better?*
8.   *Which of several equally good moves places the most stumbling blocks in my opponent's path?*
9.   *Could there be a reason for playing a second-best move in these exceptional circumstances?*
10.   *What is the very best move in this position?*
11.   *Where does each piece belong?*
12.   *What specific position would I like to obtain?*

ELEMENTARY CALCULATION

Each piece affects the game in three different ways:

1. *It embodies a quantity of force that can be employed to attain various ends.* Although this quantity may vary in exceptional circumstances, each piece has an average numerical value that is based on its general mobility. This gives us a scale of values with which to determine the desirability of a particular exchange of pieces in the vast majority of positions. The unit of valuation is the Pawn. The Bishop is worth 3; the Knight also equals 3; the Rook is worth 5, and the Queen 9. It is academic to assign the King a numerical value.

The simplest form of exchange is the capture of an *unprotected* piece.

1A

In diagram 1A, White can win a Pawn with 1 Nxe5. *The possession of an extra Pawn is sufficient to force a win in most positions.*

1B

In 1B, the Black e-pawn is attacked once and defended once. Therefore 1 Nxe5? would be a mistake, for after 1...Nxe5 Black would have a *winning material advantage* (2 units).

1C

In 1C, Black's e-pawn is attacked twice and defended once. Thus 1 Nxe5 or 1 Bxe5 wins at least a Pawn, because 1...Nxe5? would have lost material for Black when White recaptures on e5.

1D

In 1D, however, 1 Nxe5? dxe5 2 Bxe5 would leave White behind in material despite the fact that Black's e-pawn was attacked twice and defended only once.

Thus we must not only count attackers and defenders, we must also take into account the value of the pieces to be exchanged.

2. *Each piece controls squares.* The preceding examples showed that although the pieces vary in the maximum number of squares they can control, and consequently vary in value, the *quality* of their square control is exactly the same. The ability to control squares works in two ways. Expanding the number of squares that a piece controls *increases* its mobility while it *decreases* the mobility of the opponent's pieces. Compare positions 1C and 1D. In the latter, the position of Black's d-pawn on d6 restricts the mobility of White's Bishop and Knight by preventing them from capturing on e5.

3. *Each piece occupies a square.* In so doing, it *restricts the movement of any other piece* that may want to move *through* that square, (and it also *restricts the movement of any friendly piece* that may want to move *to* that square).

Every position can be seen in terms of these three interrelated *functions*. Apprehending the third is simply a matter of seeing; so is the first, once we know the scale of values. Apprehending the second, however, requires the development of a special kind of sight that can be improved with practice.

1E

In your imagination, draw a line on the board extending from White's Rook to the square a5. Also draw lines extending from the Rook to h1 and h8. Now imagine four lines, forming a square, running midway through the nine squares surrounding White's King; do the same for Black's as well. These "lines of force" cover all the squares controlled by each piece.

Even in very simple positions it would be impossible to keep track or make sense of all the criss-crossing lines of force projected by the pieces. The way to use them is to focus on only a few at a time.

In 1E, for example, you can see that White's Rook casts an impenetrable barrier around Black's King. Observe how every move of the Rook tightens the noose, by projecting the lines of force as you follow these moves:

1 Ke4 Kd6 2 Re5 Kc6 3 Rd5 Kb6 4 Kd4 Kc6 5 Kc4 Kb6 6 Rc5 Ka6 7 Rb5 Ka7 8 Kc5 Ka6 9 Kc6 Ka7 (the Black King's mobility has been reduced step-by-step) 10 Rb1 Ka8 11 Kc7 Kb8 12 Ra1 X.

The most important moves to recognize are *threats*. In 1A, White threatens Black's e-pawn. This is a *direct one-move threat*. In 1B, Black has parried the threat by defending his Pawn. In 1C, White has a *direct two-move threat*. In 1D, he has no threat at all.

There are a number of ways to parry a threat:

1. *Defend the threatened piece.*
2. *Move it away.*
3. *Capture the attacking piece.*
4. *Pin the attacking piece.*
5. *Interpose one of our pieces between the attacker and his target.*
6. *Counterattack a piece of equal or greater value (this includes checking the King).*
7. *Threaten to promote a Pawn.*

DIAGRAMS
FOR REVIEW

6

The ideal pawn structure

7

Weak squares and holes

8(W)

Capablanca-Treybal
Carlsbad 1929

9(W)

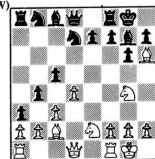

Barczay-Suttles
Sousse 1967

DIAGRAMS

10

The breakthrough

11

Opposing majorities
Crippled vs. healthy

12(W)

Nimzovich-Salve
Carlsbad 1911

13(B)
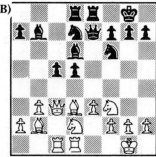

Spassky-Tal
Montreal 1979

DIAGRAMS

14(W)

Fischer-Smyslov
Havana 1965

15

Fischer-Kholmov
Havana 1965

16(B)

Tal-Georgadze
USSR 1979

17(B)

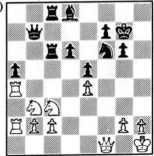

Lechtynsky-Marjanovic
Skara 1980

DIAGRAMS

18(W)

Karpov-Spassky
Montreal 1979

19(B)

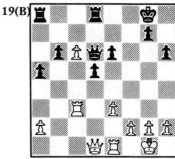

Korchnoi-Spassky
Belgrade 1977

20(W)

Korchnoi-Andersson
S. Africa 1981

21(B)

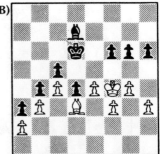

Laclau-Pytel
Val Thorens 1978

DIAGRAMS

22(W)

Rotlevy-Rubinstein
Lodz 1907

23(B)

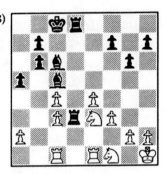

Lasker-Steinitz
1894

24(W)

Capablanca-Yates
New York 1924

25(W)

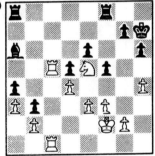

Alekhine-Yates
London 1922

DIAGRAMS

26(W)

Alekhine-Marshall
New York 1927

27(W)

Alekhine-Chajes
Carlsbad 1923

28(B)

Lewitzky-Marshall
Breslau 1912

29(W)

Tartakover-Capablanca
New York 1924

DIAGRAMS

30(W)

Capablanca-Fonaroff
New York 1918

31(B)

Watson-Grefe
USA, 1972

32(W)

Tarrasch-Marco
Vienna 1898

33(B)

Grefe-Tarjan
USA 1973

DIAGRAMS

34(B)

Bogolyubov-Alekhine
Hastings 1922

35(W)

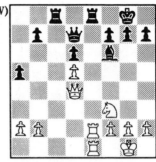

Adams-Torre
New Orleans 1920

36(B)

Reti-Alekhine
Baden-Baden 1925

37(W)

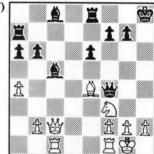

Alekhine-Rubinstein
Carlsbad 1923

DIAGRAMS

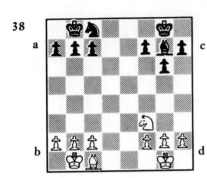

The King's fortress

The King's fortress

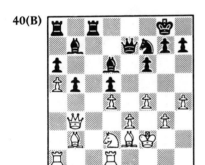

Spassky-Petrosian
Moscow 1969

Lilienthal-Ragozin
Moscow 1935

DIAGRAMS

42(B)

**Saemisch-Nimzovich
Copenhagen 1923**

43

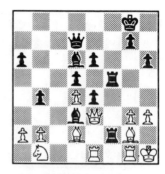

**Saemisch-Nimzovich
Copenhagen 1923**

44

Mutual Zugzwang

45(W)

**Alekhine-Nimzovich
San Remo 1930**

DIAGRAMS

46

1 e4: Classical pawn
    Skeleton

47
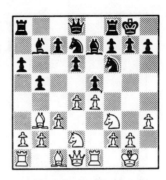

The flesh and bones
as well

48

1e4: Versus the
    hypermodern

49

The complete picture

DIAGRAMS

50

1 d4: The square d4
is the hub

51
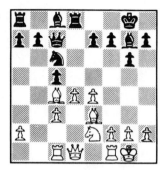

All eyes on d4

52

1 d4: A strong-point
defense

53
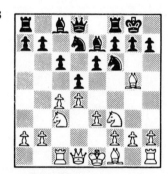

Black must
seek freedom

DIAGRAMS

54

Botvinnik-Spielmann
Moscow 1935

55(W)

1 e4 e5 2 d4
exd4 3 c3 Qe7!

56(W)

Black swallows the
"poisoned Pawn"

57(W)

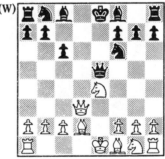

Reti-Tartakover
1910

DIAGRAMS

58(B)

Matulovic-Fischer
Vinkovci 1968

59(W)

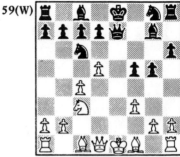

Seirawan-Browne
USA 1979

60(B)

Hamppe-Meitner
Vienna 1872

61(W)

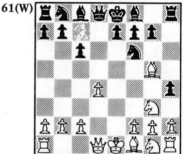

Schuster-Karls
1914

DIAGRAMS

62(B)

Larsen-Spassky
Belgrade 1970

63(W)

Zuckerman-Grefe
USA 1977

The commentary and continuations for Diagrams eight through sixty-three begin on the next page.

COMMENTARY
ON THE PRECEDING
DIAGRAMS

DIAGRAMS

8] Interlocking pawn chains; destruction of the base; open file and seventh rank; space. 40 Ral Rc8 41 Qb4 Rhd8 42 Ra7 Kf8 43 Rh1 Be8 44 Rha1 Kg8 45 R1a4 Kf8 46 Qa3 Kg8 47 Kg3 Bd7 48 Kh4 Kh8 49 Qa1 Kg8 50 Kg3 Kf8 51 Kg2 Be8 52 Nd2! Bd7 53 Nb3 Re8 54 Na5 Nd8 55 Ba6! bxa6 56 Rxd7 Re7 57 Rxd8†! Rxd8 58 Nxc6 1-0.

9] The hypermodern strategist disintegrates the chain securing White's center, then seizes the middle of the board himself. 15 Bxg7 axb2 16 Rbl Kxg7 17 cxb4 Nb6 18 Ne5 cxd4 19 Bb3? f6 20 Nd3 e5 0-1(40).

10] 1 f5, threatening 2 g5 and 3 f6. If, after 2 g5, Black plays 2... hxg5, then 3 f6. 1...b3 2 cxb3 a3 3 bxa3 c3.

11] Advancing the White kingside Pawns will produce a passed Pawn; advancing Black's queenside Pawns will not.

12] Hanging central Pawns. The blockade; siege of the backward Pawn on e6. 17...Be8 18 Rael Bxe5 19 Bxe5 Qc6 20 Bd4! Bd7 21 Qc2 Rf7 22 Re3 b6 23 Rg3 Kh8 24 Bxh7! e5! 25 Bg6! 1-0(39).

13] Dynamic potential of hanging Pawns. 15...d4! 16 exd4 cxd4 17 Qa5? Ne5 18 Nxe5 Bxe5 19 Nc4 Rd5 20 Qd2 Bxh2†! 21 Kxh2 Rh5† 22 Kg1 Ng4 0-1.

14] Doubled Pawns as static weaknesses. 34 Ne1! Ne8 35 Nd3 Nc7 36 c4! bxc4 37 Nxc4 Nb5 38 Ra6 Kf6 39 Bc1 Bb8 40 Bb2 c5 41 Nb6! Nxb6 42 Rxb6 c4 43 Nc5 c3 0-1.

15] Strength of doubled Pawns: they control key (central) squares and provide open files. 19...Nd4! 20 cxd4 exd4 21 a3 d3 22 Bxd3 Rxd3 23 Ng4 Kh7 24 e5 Nxg4 25 Qe4† g6 26 Qxg4 Rf5 0-1 (46).

16] Open files and the seventh rank. 32...Rd3!! 33 Rc8† Kh7 34 Nf8† Kh6 35 Nfd7 Rf3 36 Rh8† Kg5 37 h4† Kg4 38 Ne5† Rxe5 39 Rg8 Rxg3†! 40 fxg3 Re2† 0-1.

17] Half-open files; weak back rank. 26...Rxc3! 27 bxc3 Nxe4 28 Qf3 Rxc3! 29 Qxe4 Qxb3 30 g3 Qb1† 31 Kg2 Bb6 32 Qe2 Qg1† 33 Kh3 Re3 34 Qg2 Qd1 35 Rh4 Re2 0-1.

18] The weak isolated QP; the pin. 31 f4 f6 32 Qd1 Qb5 33 g4 g5 34 Kh1 Qc6 35 f5 Bf7 36 e4 Kg7 37 exd5 Qc7 38 Re2 b5 39 Rxe7 Rxe7 40 d6 Qc4 41 b3 1-0.

19] Rooks behind passed Pawns; the vulnerable back rank; promotion combinations. 22...Rac8 23 Qc2 e5 24 c7 Rd7 25 Rc1 d4 26 Rc6 Qd5 27 Qb1! d3 28 Qxb6 d2 29 Rd1 Qxa2 30 h3!! (30 Qb7? Qa4 31 Qxc8† Kh7 32 Qh8† Kxh8 33 c8 (Q)† Kh7 34 Rc2 Qa1!!) 30...Qa4 31 Rxd2! Rxd2 32 Qb7 Rdd8 33 cxd8 (Q)† Rxd8 34 Rc7 Qa1† 35 Kh2 e4 36 Qxe4 1-0 (48).

20] Greater freedom resulting from frontal pressure on the backward d-pawn allows lateral action and a decisive kingside attack. 23 Rd3! Bb7 24 Rg3 g6 25 Bg4! a6 26 h4 Qc5 27 h5 Qe5 28 Qd2 Bc6 29 a4 Kh8 30 hxg6 hxg6 31 Rh3† Kg8 32 Re1 Qg7 33 R1e3 Rb7 34 Rd3! Be8 35 Qg5 Nc6 36 Rh6 1-0.

21] Good vs. bad bishop; space. 1...g5† 2 Kg3 Ke5 3 Kf2 Be8 4 Kg3 Bf7 5 Kf2 (5 Be2 d3!) 5...Kf4 6 Bf1 h5 7 Bd3 Be8 8 Bf1 hxg4 9 hxg4 Ba4! 0-1.

22] The Bishops on long diagonals. Diversion, pinning. 22 g3 (22 h3 Rxc3! 23 Bxc3 Bxe4 24 Qxg4 Qxg4 25 hxg4 Rd3) 22...Rxc3! 23 gxh4 Rd2! 24 Qxd2 Bxe4† 25 Qg2 Rh3 0-1.

23] The Bishops dominate the Knights. 24...f5 25 exf5 gxf5 26 h3 Rg8 27 Nd5 Bxd5 28 cxd5 Rxd5 29 Red1 Rxd1 30 Rxd1 f4 0-1 (55).

24] A Knight's tour in practical play. 40 Nc3 Rc5 41 Ne4 Rb5 42 Ned6 Rc5 43 Nb7 Rc7 44 Nbxa5 1-0 (77).

25] The Knight rules from an invulnerable roost; the King attacks! 26 Kg3 Rfb8 27 Rc7 Bb5 28 R1c5 Ba6 29 R5c6 Re8 30 Kf4 Kg8 31 h5! Bc8 32 g3 Ba6 33 Rf7 Kh7 34 Rcc7 Rg8 35 Nd7! Kh8 36 Nf6 Rgf8 37 Rxg7! Rxe5 38 Ke5!! 1-0.

26] Pawn tension generally favors the attacker. 18 dxe5! d4 19 Qf4! dxc3 20 Qf7†! Kh8 21 bxc3! Qg8 22 Qe7 h6 23 Bh5! a5 24 e6 g6 25 exd7 Bxd7 26 Rf7 1-0.

27] Alternation; space; the pin. 63 Rh1! Nd7 64 Ra1! 1-0.

28] Surprise moves. 23...Qg3!!!

29] The Zwischenzug and the Knight fork. 9 Bxb8? Nd5! 10 Kf2 Rxb8 11 Bxc4 0-0 0-1 (30).

30] Focal points, forks, weak back ranks, the Zwischenzug, the pin (in the course of six moves!). 17 Rxd6! Rxd6 18 Bxe5 Rd1? (Black cuts his losses by 18...Qa5!) 19 Rxd1 Bxe5 20 Nh6† Kh8 21 Qxe5!! Qxe5 22 Nxf7† 1-0.

31] Diversion, interference. 33...Rad8!! 34 Bxd8 Re5!! 35 Qxe5 fxe5 36 Re2 Bxf3 37 Nxf3 Qxf3 38 Rg2 Qe3† 39 Kf1 Qd3† 40 Ke1 Qf3 0-1.

32] Space. 26 Ne6! axb3 27 axb3 Qb6 28 Nxf8 Kxf8 29 g5 hxg5 30 hxg5 Nxg5 31 Qh2 Kg8 32 Nxg5 Bxg5 33 f6 g6 34 Bxg6 1-0.

33] Perpetual check; pieces on open lines. 22...Na3†! 23 bxa3 Qb6† 24 Kc1 Qe3† 25 Kb1 ½-½.

34] Combinative Pawn promotion. 28...Nd3! 29 Rxa5 b4! 30 Rxa8 bxc3! 31 Rxe8 c2! 32 Rxf8† Kh7 33 Nf2 c1(Q)† 34 Nf1 Ne1! 35 Rh2 Qxc4 0-1 (53).

35] The weak back rank; diversion; the power of the Queen. 18 Qg4!! Qb5 19 Qc4!! Qd7 20 Qc7!! Qb5 21 a4! Qxa4 22 Re4!! Qb5 23 Qxb7!! 1-0.

36] Centralization; Rooks on open files; the initiative; forks and skewers; attack on the King; far-reaching calculation. 26...Re3! 27 Nf3 cxb5 28 Qxb5 Nc3! 29 Qxb7 Qxb7 30 Nxb7 Nxe2† 31 Kh2 Ne4! 32 Rc4! Nxf2 33 Bg2 Be6! 34 Rcc2 Ng4† 35 Kh3 Ne5† 36 Kh2 Rxf3 37 Rxe2 Ng4† 38 Kh3 Ne3† 39 Kh2 Nxc2 40 Bxf3 Nd4 0-1 (41 Rf2 Nxf3† 42 Rxf3 Bd5!).

37] The Queen effortlessly switches flanks. 21 b4! Bf8 22 Qc6 Rd7 23 g3! Qb8 24 Ng5! Red8 25 Bg6 Qe4 (25...fxg6 26 Qe4 Bxb4 27 Qh4† Kg8 28 Qh7† and mates) 26 Nxf7† 1-0 (32).

38] a & b: Solid but passive. c & d: Secure and active.

39] a: Suicidal. b: Slight compromise. c: Cause for alarm. d: A happy home.

40] A positional exchange sacrifice. 30...Rc4! 31 Qd3 Re8 32 Bf3 Bb4 33 Ba3 Bxa3 34 Rxa3 Nd6 35 Rel f5 36 Raal Ne4† 37 Bxe4 fxe4 38 Qb1 Qd7 39 Ra2 Rec8 40 Nxc4 dxc4 0-1 (56).

41] The rare double exchange sacrifice; connected passed Pawns and the initiative. 27...Rxe3!! 28 Bxe3 Rxe3 29 Nxh5 Nxh5 30 Qxh5 Bc6 31 Qg5 (31 Ra3 Re1† 32 Kh2 Qc7† 33 g3 Qe7) 31... Rxc3!! 32 Qd2 Rxc2 33 Rxc2 Ne6 34 Rd1 b4 35 Rb2 b3 0-1 (47).

42] Originality. 19...Bd6!! 20 e4 fxe4 21 Qxh5 Rxf2 22 Qg5 Raf8 23 Kh1 R8f5! 24 Qe3 Bd3! 25 Rce1 h6!!...

43] Zugzwang 0-1.

44] Whoever moves, loses.

45] Nimzovich himself Zugzwanged! The pin. 27 Ba4! b5 28 Bxb5 Ke8 29 Ba4 Kd8 30 h4!! 1-0.

46-47] 1 e4 e5 2 Nf3 Nc6 3 Bb5 a6 4 Ba4 Nf6 5 0-0 Be7 6 Re1 b5 7 Bb3 d6 8 c3 0-0 9 h3 Nb8 10 d4 Nbd7 11 Nbd2.

48-49] 1e4 Nf6 2 e5 Nd5 3 d4 d6 4 c4 Nb6 5 f4.

50-51] 1 d4 Nf6 2 c4 g6 3 Nc3 d5 4 cxd5 Nxd5 5 e4 Nxc3 6 bxc3 Bg7 7 Bc4 c5 8 Ne2 0-0 9 0-0 Nc6 10 Be3 Qc7 11 Rc1 Rd8.

52-53] 1 d4 d5 2 c4 e6 3 Nc3 Nf6 4 Bg5 Be7 5 e3 0-0 6 Nf3 Nbd7 7 Rc1 c6.

54] "Don't bring the Queen out early," say the books. 1 e4 c6 2 d4 d5 3 exd5 cxd5 4 c4 Nf6 5 Nc3 Nc6 6 Bg5 Qb6?! 7 cxd5 Qxb2??? (7...Nxd4) 8 Rc1 Na4 Qxa2 10 Bc4 Bg4 11 Nf3 Bxf3 12 gxf3 1-0.

55] Extraordinary situations require extraordinary solutions. Besides, a center Pawn is more valuable than a wing Pawn.

56] 1 e4 c5 2 Nf3 d6 3 d4 cxd4 4 Nxd4 Nf6 5 Nc3 a6 6 Bg5 e6 7 f4 Qb6! 8 Qd2 Qxb2. Masters know when to break the rules, but...

57] 1 e4 c6 2 d4 d5 3 Nc3 dxe4 4 Nxe4 Nf6 5 Qd3 e5 6 dxe5 Qa5† 7 Bd2 Qxe5 8 0-0-0! Nxe4? (8...Be7) 9 Qd8†!! Kxd8 10 Bg5†, and mate by either 11 Rd8 or 11 Bd8. ... sometimes even they must play the fools.

58] The fighting King. 10...b4 11 Nd5 Nxd5 12 Qxd5 Rb8 13 Bxe7 Kxe7!! 14 Qd2 Nf6 15 Bg2 Bb7 16 Qd3 Qb6 0-1 (40).

59] The foolhardy King. 10 Kd2!? Nd4! 11 Bd3 Kd8! 12 Ng1! b5! 13 Nge2 (13 cxb5) 13...bxc4 14 Bxc4 Qc5! 15 Kd3? (Delusions of grandeur.) 15...Rb8 16 Be3? Qxc4†! 17 Kxc4 Ba6† 18 Nb5 Nxb5! 0-1.

60] A forced march. (1 e4 e5 2 Nc3 Bc5 3 Na4?! Bxf2†!? 4 Kxf2 Qh4† 5 Ke3 Qf4† 6 Kd3 d5 7 Kc3 Qxe4 8 Kb3 Na6 9 a3) 9... Qxa4†!! 10 Kxa4 Nc5† 11 Kb4 a5†!! 12 Kxc5 Ne7 (threatening 13...b6† 14 Kb5 Bd7 X) 13 Bb5†! Kd8 14 Bc6! b6†! 15 Kb5 Nxc6 16 Kxc6 Bb7†! 17 Kb5 Ba6† 18 Kc6! (18 Ka4?? Bc4 and 19...b5 X) 18...Bb7†! ½-½.

61] The passed Pawn in the opening! Black breaks all the rules; The Zwischenschach. (1 e4 c6 2 d4 d5 3 Nc3 dxe4 4 Nxe4 Nf6 5 Ng3 h5 6 Bg5? [6 h4] 6...h4) 7 Bxf6 hxg3! 8 Be5 Rxh2! 9 Rxh2 Qa5†! 10 c3 (10 Qd2 gxf2†) 10...Qxe5†!! 11 dxe5 gxh2 0-1.

62] The passed Pawn again. 12...h4!! 13 hxg4 hxg3 14 Rg1 Rh1! 15 Rxh1 g2 16Rf1 Qh4† 17 Kd1 gxf1(Q)† 0-1.

63] The passed Pawn in the middlegame; weak back rank. 28 b4!? e4!! (the only move) 29 Rh3 (threatening 30 Rxh7) 29...e3!! 30 bxc5 Qd2 31 Qa1 e2 32 Kg1 Qd1! 33 Qxd1 exd1(Q) 34 Rxd1 Rxd1† 0-1 (43).

SUPPLEMENTARY
LIST I

I: The Immortals and Their Games

The immortals naturally excel at all types of positions, but each stamps his games with a very special mark.

1. *Botvinnik: 100 Selected Games*   Botvinnik; Dover
2. *Capablanca's 100 Best Games of Chess*   Golombek; McKay
3. *From My Chess Games: 1920-1937*   Euwe; Dover
4. *My 60 Memorable Games*   Fischer; Simon & Schuster
5. *Bobby Fischer's Chess Games*   Wade & O'Connell; Doubleday
6. *Karpov's Collected Games*   Levy; RHM
7. *Korchnoi's 400 Best Games*   Korchnoi, Wade, Blackstock; Arco
8. *Larsen's Selected Games of Chess*   Larsen; Bell & Hyman
9. *Lasker's Greatest Chess Games: 1899-1914*   Reinfeld & Fine; Dover
10. *Marshall's Best Games of Chess*   Marshall; Dover
11. *Morphy's Games of Chess*   Sergeant; Dover
12. *Chess Praxis*   Nimzovich; Dover
13. *Tigran Petrosian: His Life and Games*   Vasiliev; RHM
14. *Pillsbury's Chess Career*   Sergeant & Watts; Dover
15. *Selected Games of Lajos Portisch*   Varnusz; Arco
16. *Reshevsky's Best Games of Chess*   Reshevsky; Dover
17. *Reti's Best Games of Chess*   Reti & Golombek; Dover
18. *Rubinstein's Chess Masterpieces*   Kmoch; Dover
19. *My Best Games of Chess: 1935-1957*   Smyslov; Dover
20. *Spassky's 100 Best Games*   Cafferty; Batsford
21. *The Chess Career of Rudolf Spielmann*   Spence; The Chess Player
22. *Wilhelm Steinitz: Selected Chess Games*   Devide; Dover
23. *Life and Games of Mikhail Tal*   Tal; RHM
24. *Complete Games of Mikhail Tal* (Four Volumes)   Thomas; Arco
25. *Tarrasch's Best Games of Chess*   Reinfeld; Dover

103

SUPPLEMENTARY
LIST II

II: For the Rabid Reader

1. *How to Play the Sicilian Defense* Levy & O'Connell; McKay
   A model approach to the study of a complex opening. Out
   of print.
2. *Guide to the Chess Openings* Barden & Harding; McKay
3. *How to Play the Openings in Chess* Keene & Levy; RHM
4. *An Opening Repertoire
   for the Attacking Player* Keene & Levy; Batsford
5. *An Opening Repertoire for Black* Marovic & Parma; Arco
6. *The Chess Opening for You* Evans; RHM
   A repertoire for those pressed for time.
7. *The Openings in Modern Theory and Practice* Keene;
   Bell & Hyman
8. *The Middle Game, I & II* Euwe & Meiden; Bell & Hyman
   Classics covering similar material to Pachman's
   middlegame works.
9. *My System* Nimzovich; McKay
   A brilliant pioneering work that provided a number of
   today's top grandmasters with their first insights
   into the mysteries of chess strategy,
10. *The Art of the Middlegame* Keres & Kotov; Penguin
    The chapters on defending difficult positions and
    analyzing adjourned games are outstanding. Out of print.
11. *How to Play the Middlegame in Chess* Littlewood; Collins
    Thought-provoking, instructive and entertaining.
12. *The game of Chess* Tarrasch; McKay
    Delightful, comprehensive manual for novices and
    slightly more advanced players; first published in 1931.
13. *Tal's Winning Chess Combinations* Tal & Khenkin;
    Simon & Schuster
    Amusing instruction. Lots of key patterns and exercises.
14. *Play for Mate* Hooper & Cafferty; McKay
    Mating patterns illustrated by nearly three hundred
    examples.

15. *New Ideas in Chess*　　　　　　　　　　Evans;
　　　A candid revelation of a tough, pragmatic chess
　　　philosophy. Out of print.
16. *Modern Ideas in Chess*
　　　and Masters of the Chessboard　　　　　Reti; Dover
　　　Enduring studies of chess evolution, the precursors of
　　　the following book —
17. *The Battle of Chess Ideas*　　　　　　　Saidy; RHM
　　　Lyric, philosophical and intensely human look at ten
　　　of today's top chess players and their influence
　　　on the game.
18. *Chess from Morphy to Botvinnik*　　　Konig; Bonanza
　　　A century of chess traced in the games of the greats
　　　through their approach to thematic middlegames.
　　　Out of print.
19. *The Art of Defense in Chess*　　　　　Soltis; McKay
　　　Excellent. The most complete coverage ever of a
　　　difficult topic.
20. *The King-Hunt in Chess*　　　　　　　Cozens; Dover
　　　45 games illustrating the many ways to hunt down
　　　the King.
21. *The Chess Sacrifice*　　　　　　　　　Vukovic; Bell
　　　A masterpiece equal in stature to "The Art of Attack
　　　in Chess." Out of Print.
22. *Analyzing the Endgame*　　　　　　　Speelman; Arco
　　　Penetrating analysis for advanced players.
23. *Predicament in Two Dimensions*　　Mengarini; Thinker's Press
　　　An experienced master and practicing psychologist
　　　inquires into many aspect of practical play.
24. *Modern Chess Brilliancies*　　　　　　Evans; Fireside
　　　What is a brilliancy? Clear, precise notes.
25. *Modern Chess Miniatures*　　Barden & Heidenfeld; Dover
　　　Varied and entertaining. How not to become a victim.
26. *The Art of Chess Analysis*　　　　　　Timman; RHM
　　　Does not teach chess analysis, but examines 24 great
　　　battles in depth.

27. *Second Piatigorsky Cup*   Kashdan; Dover
    One of the strongest tournaments ever held, with most
    of the games containing candid annotations by both
    players.
28. *Montreal 1979*   Tal, Chepizhny, Roshal; Pergamon
    Incredibly strong double round robin. Great human
    interest material, many games annotated by the players
    themselves or top grandmasters.
29. *The World Chess Championship*   Gligoric & Wade; RHM
    Every game played in world championship encounters
    since 1948, many of them annotated. Introductory
    comments on each match by Gligoric.
30. *How to Get the Most*
    from Your Chess Computer   Kaplan; RHM
    International master and computer specialist who designed
    various chess playing programs talks about man versus
    machine and machines helping man.
31. *Players Chess News*
    A bi-weekly newspaper containing approximately 100
    important and interesting games every issue, delivered
    less than a month after they have been played. Also
    news and theoretical articles.

ANSWERS
TO THE STUDY QUIZZES
IN THE "THIRTY-FIVE
BEST BOOKS"

ANSWERS

Understanding the Open Games: 1) f2 and f7. 2) rapid; direct; 3) gambit. 4) accept. 5) return the material at the proper moment. 6) decline. 7) attack; evaporate. 8) center; kingside. 9) symmetry. 10) temperament.

Art of Chess Combination: 1) Forcing. It limits and directs the opponent's moves. 2) Surprise and risk. 3) Our opponent can move only one piece in his attempts to meet it. 4) superior positions.

Essential Knowledge: 1) A Rook. 2) A blockade. 3) Active Kings, reduced material, the fight to queen a passed Pawn. 4) Reduce it to a simpler, known case. 5) The properties of the individual pieces and the ways to coordinate them are more easily grasped in simple positions. 6) 1. Deploy the pieces to maximum effect (usually through centralization); 2. Provoke weaknesses in the opposing pawn structure; 3. Advance the Pawn so the opponent will have to sacrifice a piece for it, or blockade it while leaving the other wing open to invasion. 4. In the latter case, switch to the opposite wing and capture enough Pawns so that one of your own must eventually queen.

Logical Chess Move by Move: 1) The King's Bishop. 2) No. 3) No. A closed central position justifies a wing attack. 4) By a counterattack in the center. 5) It doesn't fit in with Black's plan, surrenders the center, and wastes time by capturing a Pawn that his opponent will easily recover. 6) e4. 7) It loses material after 6...Nxd5! 7 Bxd8 Bb4†. 8) By playing ...d5 and ...c5 with impunity. 9) The c-file.

Ideas Behind the Chess Openings: a)7M b)9L c)8D d)18C e)11E f)13O g)15N h)12Q i)16A j)17T k)14S l)3F m)2G n)20I o)1H p)6R q)5K r)4P s)19J t)10B

ANSWERS

How to Play Chess Endings: 1) Stalemate; perpetual check; eliminating the last Pawn. 2) Pawns; Kings; reversal. 3) The struggle revolving around the queening of a passed Pawn. 4) Rook. 5) The Rook. 6) "bad". 7) The Bishop is a long-range piece, the Knight is not; the Knight can cover squares of both colors, the Bishop cannot. 8) White wins, because the "rule of the square" applies from his third rank. 9) The outside passed Pawn.

Judgment and Planning in Chess: 1) Through the process of drawing conclusions in practical play. 2) critical position. 3) Won games will not win themselves. We must still think and make the pieces work for us. 4) We can: Compare positions with similar ones that we already know well. Weigh the elements and outstanding features affecting each player's position. Work out more or less forced variations till we reach a clarified position that allows us to formulate a quick, definite conclusion, such as White has a winning material advantage, etc. 5) We must procede from generalities to specifics and, in the end, evaluate each position on its own merits. 6) The smaller number of Pawns makes it easier to generate a passed Pawn, and the general advance necessary for this does not endanger the King. In the endgame, this Pawn is far from the enemy King. 7) latent potential. 8) One type of advantage can be converted into another. 9) second weakness. 10) less; more. 11) carefully prepared. Otherwise the Pawns will become weak. 12) In order to eradicate weak moves from our play, we must pinpoint the source of errors.

A Complete Defense: 1) Counterattack. 2) Because of the absence of central pawn tension and the complex problems it brings. 3) So that White cannot castle on the opposite wing in order to initiate a pawn storm. 4) d5. 5) It opens the position when White is ahead in development. 6) White will gain an advantage by a double

ANSWERS

attack against d5 and b7. 7) It restrains Black's queenside ambitions, and the QR may come into play via a3. It fails to develop a piece and weakens the square b4. 8) The one arising after 1 d4 d5 2 c4 dxc4 3 Nf3 Nf6 4 e3 Bg4 5 Bxc4 e6 6 h3 Bh5 7 Nc3 Nbd7 8 0-0 Bd6 9 e4 e5 9) After 4 Nc3, White's gambit has become a real one. 10) transposition; move-order.

Modern Chess Tactics: 1)crisis; initiative; radical. 2) belief; infallibility. 3) order. 4) active; passive; waiting. 5) Tactical coordination; strength.

Modern Chess Strategy: 1) The static and the dynamic. 2) Positions must be analyzed and evaluated. 3) A good Bishop is one that is unobstructed by its own Pawns, a bad Bishop is the reverse. 4) They encourage an attack on the King. 5) The Knight. 6) They are brought to the central files, which are usually the first to be opened. Advancing the RP's and lifting the Rooks into play along the third rank is hazardous, because they can easily come under attack by the Bishops and Knights. 7) defense. 8) The Knight. 9) Their advance usually opens the game favorably for the side possessing one. The isolated QP supports the outpost squares at Bishop five and King five, and the latter often provides the impetus for a kingside attack. The Pawn's inherent weakness becomes more noticeable as pieces are exchanged. 10) The defender cannot keep up with his oppenent's alternating maneuvers against them due to the passive placement of his pieces. 11) To prevent it from being easily driven away. 12) positional superiority.

The Art of Attack in Chess: 1) Action. 2) Understanding the correct launching of an attack. 3) along; e-file. 4) pin. 5) Obtaining the maximum preconditions for an attack with the minimum of

ANSWERS

commitment. 6) mating square; focal-points. 7) passive. 8) focal-point. 9) The opening of the center or the other wing.

Pawn Structure Chess: 1) Black's position is solid but somewhat passive, as he lacks a pawn foothold in the center. White has outposts at c5 and e5, and a piece posted on the latter provides the positional justification for an attack on the King. Black cannot af-afford to remain totally passive, and should try to free his game with ...e5 or ...c5. ...c5 can often leave Black on the wrong side of an inferior endgame if White emerges with a 3:2 queenside majority. 2) d5. 3) central pawn majority. 4) strong cramping effect. 5) its base. 6) The base is the most vulnerable link in the chain. 7) The same structures arise in a number of different openings. 8) Hanging Pawns, the isolated QP, and the minority attack. 9) c4.

Modern Chess Opening Theory: 1) Control of the center. 2) Building a pawn center. Tearing it down. 3) on; central; occupying. 4) Pieces posted in the center control a greater number of squares than those on the wing. They can be easily shifted to a critical flank. 5) concrete approach. 6) dynamic; static. 7) counterplay! 8) positional; forced tactical. 9) static weaknesses; active. 10) the middlegame arising logically from it. 11) concrete plan; middlegame 12) The central Pawns quickly disappear in most of the open games, leaving few difficult problems to be solved whereas the central pawn tension in the Ruy persists for a long time. 13) it can be supported by pieces; the opponent has no chance of creating effective pressure against it. 14) strong pawn center (see pg. 37 in *MCOT*). 15) initiative. 16) classify.

Basic Chess Endings: 1) the easiest to win. 2) the rule of the square, the opposition, triangulation, key squares, reserve pawn

ANSWERS

tempi, passed Pawns protecting one another, the King's "circular" route. 3) gain; tempo. 4) of the wrong color. 5) Rook Pawns. 6) off; same-colored. 7) a Pawn. 8) perpetual check. 9) Queen endgames. 10) Pawns. 11) pawn. 12) exchange pieces. 13) wind up with all the Pawns on one side of the board.

Think, Train, Play Like a Grandmaster: 1) a. He reckons the material situation. b. Asks himself if he's seen the position before. c. Take account of the position's main features. d. Draws up a plan. e. Analyzes variations and evaluates their resulting positions. f. Chooses a move. 2) analyze; only once. 3) too many; too few. 4) No. Black has a draw in variation B4. 5) Selectivity, speed, and accuracy. 6) forced; unforced. 7) direct; forcing. 8) A move singled out for further investigation during the search for a move. 9) single candidate. 10) blind spot. 11) conditioned reflex. 12) Single and multi-stage. 13) Well-annotated games. 14) economical; thinking time. 15) annotate; deeply; objectively.

Grandmaster Preparation: 1) We must be systematic and thorough, and avoid the tendency to make premature judgments. 2) "Play what you know best." 3) motivation.